Oops,
I Broke A Nail!

DIG YOURSELF FREE FROM PAST
HURT, DISCOVER YOUR TRUE
SELF-WORTH

Collena R. Doctor

DAYELight
PUBLISHERS

Book Cover Design by HCP Book Publishing

ISBN: 978-1-949343-23-6

Table of Contents

ACKNOWLEDGMENTS

I don't remember the exact age that it happened, but ever since I was a little girl, I always knew that I was supposed to write a book — the 'when and how' I didn't know. I didn't even take this nagging desire seriously, but I always knew. Now that it's here, I know that the day God planted the desire in my heart was the day each chapter of the book began writing itself.

The first person I want to thank is my Lord and Saviour, Jesus Christ. As I scrolled through endless pictures on social media sites, lying on my couch feeling particularly sorry for myself, wallowing in my own self-pity, I heard a soft voice in my head saying, "It's time," and just like that, I got up and took the first step and opened my laptop. I want to thank God for always being my pillar of strength and my fortress. He is the One I can run to when no man will understand what I am going through and how to fix it. God loves me so much that through writing this book, I have experienced so much healing of wounds I didn't know I still had, and He loves you so much that He would use my story to help you save yourself the hurt and learn from someone else's experience.

Then there is my mother, Maureen A. O'Connor. In high school, we read a poem in Literature class that I always loved, "For my Mother, May I Inherit Half Her Strength." That title is so befitting of the way I feel about my mother. From day one, Mom, you would give me your last dollar, even though for you, it meant doing without. Thank you for telling me no as even when it made me mad – it kept me safe. Thank you for sticking around, even when others threw in the towel. Your love for and dedication to all your children and your insistence on honesty and integrity has left an indelible mark on my life, one that can never be erased. You are the epitome of a queen, and I love you more than I can try to say here.

To my husband, Dain, thank you for your undying support of all the antics that I am always up to. For keeping our very clingy daughter away from me so that I can enjoy the simple joys of sleeping. For babysitting on a regular basis and keeping this boat afloat without complaint so that I can work, study, write and do all the things I needed to do to make this book a success. Thank you for always lending me your shoulder when I needed a good place to cry. I love you, and I could not have done this without you. Thank you.

A big thank you to the team at DayeLight Publishers, and especially to the COO and Founder, and my amazing book coach, Crystal Daye. You have been to me nothing short of patient, kind, honest, and a great coach and friend. I remember asking God to please direct me to the people that He wanted to publish this book, and He led me to you. Thank you for your obedience to God, and for the amazing work that you did for me, are doing for this country, and are doing for this world at large. May God continue to bless you DayeLight Publishers.

And last, but most definitely not least, I want to thank my sisters, brothers, closest cousins, in-laws, and my very few, very best friends. You have all played such a dynamic role in who I was, to becoming who I am today and have helped set the premise for this book. Thank you for sticking by me, even when I messed up. I am far from perfect, though I sometimes try, but thank you for letting me know it's okay not to be and for loving me just as I am.

FOREWORD

It is an awesome privilege to write the foreword for *Oops, I Broke A Nail! Dig Yourself Free from Past Hurt, Discover Your True Self Worth*, an awe-inspiring anecdote that chronicles the life of a young entrepreneur and an aspiring life coach who continues to defy the odds. Born in a volatile community located in the city of Kingston, Jamaica, Collena is no stranger to the realities of father absenteeism, single motherhood, peer pressure, poverty and the stigmas associated with living in a garrison community. Sadly, some of these realities are currently being lived by hundreds of thousands of teenagers across the globe which is part of the reason Collena felt it necessary to document her story knowing that her testimony of trials and triumphs would dramatically change someone's life.

Important to note, however, is the remedial role the Holy Spirit has played and continues to play in her life which is the reason she attributes her victories not to her own strength or the strength of any human being, but rather to a tight-knit relationship she was able to develop with her Lord and Saviour, Jesus Christ of Nazareth. Her zeal and infectious love for the Lord is what had drawn a sinner like me to Christ who through His grace has taught me what it really means to be loved.

Collena's relationship with Jesus emerged out of a place of brokenness and vulnerability, the kind of situation that would seemingly deprive one of certain opportunities that are considered pre-requisites for success. However, God was going to turn those situations around for her good as a testament to Genesis 50:20a which reads:

*But as for you, ye thought evil against me;
but God meant it unto good...*

So, needless to say, all the rejection this woman of God has suffered in her past have worked together for a greater good which is her finding acceptance, love, joy and the peace of God that surpasseth all understanding.

Oops, I Broke a Nail! is not an apologetic but it is rather a manifesto of perseverance, triumph, and determination that you too can adopt to bring out the best in you even if it means getting bruised along the way. See, the beauty of it all is that although you might get bruised, you will still get over it and although you will risk losing some things, God's grace is sufficient to restore. Isn't that awesome? What a mighty God we serve! No wonder Chapter 4 is easily my favourite chapter of the book, and I wouldn't be surprised if it turns out to be yours too. Don't worry, if you are a new convert growing up in a city as busy as Kingston and one that is heavily influenced by the lifestyle in Hollywood, you will know just what I'm talking about.

As a matter of fact, in most societies, if not all, you may find that sin usually abounds. But guess what?

"...where sin abounded, grace did much more abound." (Romans 5:20).

To further qualify this point, you will soon realize that one of the most common patterns portrayed in this narrative is the cycle of falling into sin and then being redeemed by God's grace. It is important to note that this very pattern embodies the true essence of *Oops, I Broke a Nail!* as it highlights the redemptive and restorative power of the Holy Spirit that is available for all those who call upon Him.

I truly hope you are already intrigued by the lessons this powerful book has to teach you as you prepare to follow your dreams. I believe your life will never be the same after reading it. I believe you are going to be empowered so much so you will quit making excuses. Yes, allow that broken relationship that you have with your father (or mother) to push you to try a little harder and let those negative words give you all the more reasons to prove your doubters wrong. What am I saying? If there was ever a time when you ought to be stepping out by faith, that time is now, even if it means breaking a nail.

Sharnadeen S. Anglin (Ms.)
Minister
Author of *Since I've Seen Jesus*
Founder of www.iveseenjesus.com
Freelance Writer
Broadcaster at TBC Radio

PREFACE

In high school, I was the kind of girl who could not learn anything in class until my face was washed cooler than a winter's breeze and my lips were shining like the sun from my newest lip gloss. I loved to get A's in school, but that was not good enough for me – I wanted to look good while I got good grades. 'Pretty dunce' was never a term that could describe me, and I made sure of it. It was my great joy and pleasure to show all the onlookers that you didn't have to look like a frumpy nerd to be good at the books, and if you looked pretty, your head didn't have to be empty either. I enjoyed – and still do – looking good.

Then there is my fighting personality, from the playground to the workplace. I was never afraid to give a punch or two to the girl – or boy – who would dare come and mess with me. On top of all that, who in their right minds would go to the defense of total strangers who were being unfairly treated or spoken down to? I would take on battles that were not my own and fight them as if I were Martin Luther King Jr. reincarnated. When in a meeting with all my colleagues and something important but hard had to be said to Management, they all looked at me and said, "Collena, say it." I have never backed down when it came to justice and fair treatment.

Because growing up was tough, I have learned to become a fighter. The title of this book was born out of those experiences. It is unfortunate that so many of us die without living up to our fullest potential because of the bad situations in our past that never seemed to let us go. That is why, at the end of this book, you will understand that the people and the situations that have held you down for so long will not just hand you a 'get out of jail free' card, you will have to fight for that freedom, and I am here to help you do it.

Over the years, I have grown in wisdom, and though I now choose my battles very carefully, I am still not shy about rolling up my sleeves, messing up my manicure, and going to war, but not a physical war – I fight in the Spirit. Thankfully, I now understand that no matter who the representative is at any given time, the true enemy is always the devil – he just uses different masks and faces in each battle. At the end of this book, you too will learn how to fight the right way – in the Spirit. You see, when you fight physically, with your fists and your words, you will always be fighting the same battles. When you learn to fight in the Spirit, with prayer and declarations of *the* Word, which is sharper than any two-edged sword, you will always win the war.

CHAPTER 1

DUMPED

The ground was cold and hard. I could feel the dusty grain sink into my skin as my knees hit the dirty surface. It took my brain only a second to register what was happening as I dived under the table along with my brothers and sisters. In rapid fire, I heard the bullets leave the gun, and their explosive sound rang in my ears. To be honest, I don't remember much of the details of that night, but what I do remember clearly is the fear – the fear of dying, the fear of someone I knew dying, pure, undiluted fear. I covered my ears tightly with my hands as I noticed that the fear had my brother and sisters in the same grip that it had me. Moments passed like years as we waited for the gunshots to stop. I didn't know it then, but what I would come to know as 'get flat' would be a regular occurrence for me.

Growing up in the volatile area of "Maxfield Bottom," as we called it, was an experience for me. One that, when I look back now, had God written all over it. My mother was a single parent who worked extremely long hours as a Security Officer, or Security Guard as we called it then, and after she – very wisely if you ask me – fled from August Town and the perpetually pounding fist of my abusive father, she settled with us on Pretoria Road, off Maxfield Avenue. I didn't know it then, but that was the first time I felt dumped. The rent was cheap, along with a lot of other factors, and not very nice ones at that. First, we lived in what was called a 'tenement yard.' There were at least four different families sharing one yard and one bathroom, which was located outside. There was no light in the bathroom structure either, so if you missed the sunlight and was not showered by the time mommy got home, "dog nyam yu supper," as we would say in Jamaica. What that phrase simply meant was, darkness or not, centipedes or not, midnight or not, you were going outside to have your shower. At night, the water was freezing cold, and if we were ever so unlucky to have any of the other tenants using the water in their house while we were showering, the soap would dry on our skin, because the water pressure was only strong enough to service one household at a time.

Growing up with my single mother, an older brother and sister, and one younger sister had its ups and downs. To my young mind, my mother was constantly quarrelling about something. My siblings and I would whisper about her behind her back about how miserable she was. As children, we were not the most well-behaved, obedient children, and my mother was not afraid to get the switch, belt, shoes, board, you name it. There were times when she was beating us, and you could tell that she was going through a rough time. It was as though she was taking out her frustration on us as she beat us.

I can honestly say Mother did her best. Looking back now on all the things I used to think and even say, I wish I could take them back. I was ungrateful, as children can sometimes be, and in the early years, I could never understand why every child always seemed to have more than I had. I struggled through those feelings all the way up to the sixth grade.

In starting my first primary school at the age of six, I was excited. I looked forward to going to school every day. I felt safe, like I belonged there. I loved to learn, and although I didn't know it then, God had given me special abilities to rise above any dumping ground. I would soon cop the certificate for the most outstanding child in Grade One, coming first in my class. I continued on to Grade Two at Melrose Primary & Junior High School, but as that school was on a shift system, I was placed on the evening shift. School began for me in the afternoon. As a young girl, whose mother had to leave for work early each morning, it was not safe to leave me at home alone until the afternoon. She would ask my father – who was a taxi driver at the time – to come and pick me up and take me to school. The funny thing is that I don't remember him being dependable even then. He must not have been consistent because one day, while I crossed the street as a six- or seven-year-old child, a driver hit me on the pedestrian crossing. Thank goodness he wasn't speeding, and it was only a little bruise. Why would I be crossing the street if my father was supposed to take me to school each day? It was from that early age that I started thinking maybe my daddy was not as nice as I thought he was. That accident scared my mother into swiftly moving me from that school and placing me in Rousseau Primary School, a school without a shift system.

Upon entering my new school in the middle of the school year, they didn't have any space for me, and they probably didn't want to enrol me either. But, of course, no one wants to tell a desperate mother no, as she will only keep coming back. So, naturally, they dumped me again by placing me in the class with the slowest, noisiest, most troublesome students in the second grade. I knew that was not where I belonged, but what could I do? My mother was just glad they had agreed to take me in.

Luke 11:33 reminds us that:

No man, when he hath lighted a candle, putteth it in a secret place, neither under a bushel, but on a candlestick, that they which come in may see the light.

God had lit a light in me, and no matter how hard the enemy tried to hide me, my light would always shine. After a short time in the slowest class, my teacher *had to* move me into class one, where the brightest children were. Class one was so full that I didn't have my own space to sit. I was propped up against a full desk of students on a chair that was mostly in the walkway. Looking back now, that teacher had no choice, as it was written:

Ye are the light of the world. A city that is set on an hill cannot be hid. (Matthew 5:14)

"Stretch out your hands!" Shouted my teacher, as she firmly placed the ruler in the palm of my red hands. I, along with another girl, was being punished for fighting in school. I got picked on a lot, though I'm not sure why, but I was a fighter, and no one who crossed me got away with it. Now that I think about it, children who grow up getting a beating for any and almost everything lived very defensive lives even from an early age. I was angry most of the time, although I tried to hide it. I couldn't quite understand why my father would beat down the door, threatening to hurt my mother if she didn't return the stove she had 'stolen' when she left him. I didn't understand why the police was at our house, and I surely didn't understand why every afternoon, while all the other children went home, I had to sit on the side of the road with my younger sister, waiting for hours until my father decided or remembered to pick us up from school. We would sit, as two young children, on an old, dirty light-post that had fallen, until the sun said goodbye and the moon smiled hello. It was such an embarrassing time in our lives, as we watched all our classmates and teacher make their way home while we sat there on the street.

My mother moved again to Vineyard Town when Maxfield Avenue got too dangerous for us to live comfortably. She worked such long hours, she could no longer leave her four children home alone to look after each other. My father's only responsibility was to pick us up from school and take us home. We were still too young to take the bus home. He failed at that too. Many nights his taxi colleagues would see us sitting on the side of the road and offer to take us to him. Looking back now, there must have been angels watching over us. We did not recognize those 'friends' of his, but we were two tired, and hungry little girls who desperately wanted to go home. Thankfully, those men who sometimes rescued us from the sad stares of passers-by did take us to our father, holed up in the gambling shop at Maxfield Bottom. When his fellow taxi driver dropped us off, he had no apology for us, not even a look of remorse. He would offer to buy us some snacks and tell us to sit in his car and wait. Then he would go back inside to gamble for hours until he decided to leave, or his money was finished, whichever came first. Now, I can only imagine how worried sick my mother must have been. I learned later in life that my father didn't take my mother's calls, and when he did, he would use profane language before hanging up on her. If that wasn't bad enough, after leaving the gambling shop, usually after quarrelling and waving his knife at someone who declared that he couldn't leave just yet, he would put us in the trunk of his taxi while he ran a few more trips to 'make up our lunch money' as he would call it. Sometimes, we didn't get home until after nine o'clock at night, or probably later. During those many days and nights of our father forgetting us on the street and putting us in the trunk of his car to make room for his passengers, the admiration and adoration a little girl naturally has for her father started to leave me.

My mother, for as long as I have known her, has been a worrier, and so, no matter how badly our father treated us after school, the arrangement didn't change. We were to still wait on him after school each day. I guess she felt we were safer there than if we were to take the bus home by ourselves. But one fateful day, my sister Collette, who is two years younger than I, had a bad case of diarrhea. Before this, whenever she or I needed to use the bathroom while waiting for our father, we would go and borrow the bathroom of a nearby bar. However, that evening I had had enough, and I decided that we were going to take the bus by ourselves and go home so that she could use the bathroom properly. We got home safely, but when my mother called my father to find out if he had us and he declared that we were not at our usual spot, she had a fit. When she got home and saw us there safe and sound, she gave me a fine beating for taking the bus alone. Man, she beat me so badly; she dissolved all her worry and frustration into each lashing. After that day and that beating, she decided we were sensible enough to take the bus home alone.

So yes, I would fight at school because children are naïve and innocent, and that makes them cruel when it comes to teasing other children. I would get teased about being left on the side of the road every day, about the fact that I only had one suit of clothes to wear every time we had an out-of-uniform day at school, and because I never seemed to have enough, if any, lunch money. One day, this boy told the whole class that I had kissed him for ten dollars. They laughed and teased me to scorn. I vehemently denied it and cried and ran away, but though I am feeling a bit coy, I can now confess that it was actually the truth. Boy, that taught me an important lesson, in the harshest way; never beg for money, and never trust a boy who says he will give only if you kiss him, but he won't tell.

Not having enough to eat or matching clothes to wear were things that I couldn't control, but children don't know that, so they mocked me endlessly. When I ignored them, they hit me and threw things at me. From an early age, I had a short temper, and once it flared, there was no stopping me. I loved to wear very long nails, and whenever I fought with anyone, they would bear those scars for a while to come. Throughout all of that, God's Spirit of excellence was upon me. I was a bright student, troubled, mouthy, and loved to fight, but I was an A student. And it was for this very reason that, although my mother owed many weeks of extra lesson fees, my gracious sixth-grade teacher still allowed me to take extra lessons and Saturday classes. I did extremely well in school and passed my Primary School exams to move on to the first school I fell in love with, Holy Childhood High School.

A Lesson Learned in the Rain

I don't know how men abandon their children and do not know or care to know if they are eating or even alive yet have the audacity to boast when they have achieved something. That was my father. Until I took my school exit exams, my father had become more and more distant. My younger sister and I got used to the sound of his voicemail, "Please leave your name and number...." Sometimes we would leave messages that usually sounded like this, "Daddy, can you please come? We are hungry." Yet daddy didn't come. It got to the point where, as eleven and nine-year-old girls, we started to realize that if we allowed caller ID to show, then he didn't pick up, but if we blocked the caller ID, he always answered. I knew he didn't want to talk to us. On those occasions where he unknowingly picked up our private call, he would say, "Ok, I am coming," then we would wait for hours until we finally accepted that he wasn't coming. Then there were the times he actually did show up. He would bring some groceries and sometimes cash and never stayed for more than five minutes at a time. Then there were the nights he dropped by the house very late at night, like midnight or even later, to drop off our 'lunch money' for school. My mother hated being disturbed from her sleep because she worked more than twelve hours daily to feed us, but she would still drag herself out of bed, as we needed whatever money he brought. The money my father brought was never enough and was usually completely spent after we bought breakfast, but to give him his due, he did try. He just didn't try his best.

With all that happening for a while, I was now moving on to a prestigious high school, one of the best. When my father heard the news, he showed me off to his fellow taxi confederates, boasting that I was his daughter, and I just passed for Holy Childhood. Even as a child, I was disgusted at what he was doing, knowing the truth of the story.

The day came when it was time to do my medical examinations to enter the school. The cost was five thousand Jamaican dollars, and my mother had been asking my father for assistance for weeks. He didn't come through for us, and my mother, as she always did in her superhuman way, managed to come up with the exact amount. It was the final week before school opened, and the exam could not be put off any longer. My mother warned before we left the house that morning, "Collena, I only have one hundred dollars for our bus fare. No more to buy food or for the bus fare home. I have asked your father to pick us up after the exam is over." The area where my father operated his taxi was about a minute's walk from my new school, and I thought, "Okay, no problem." Except, this was my father, and we called him about ten times before he finally decided to answer. His response was that he was nowhere near that location and couldn't help us. With a click of his phone, indicating the end of the call, we made our way home, on foot. I will never forget that day because it was one of the hallmarks of my life and was the beginning of the woman I am today. Modern research confirms that the distance from my school to our home in Vineyard Town is a little over 5 kilometres and it would take 120 minutes to complete the journey walking. It must have taken us almost two hours to walk all the way home, and if that wasn't bad enough, it began to rain heavily halfway through our journey.

My mother had runner's itch, a condition where the capillaries and arteries in the leg expand because the body is not used to exercise, causing a sensation that our brains read as itchiness. This can sometimes also occur because of the material of the clothing we are wearing coupled with the sweat we produce during exercise. The rain was pouring and my mother began scratching at her thighs wildly. We stopped in the rain, as there was no shelter, as she scratched and dug at her skin like a wildcat. I was twelve years old, and obviously naïve, because I started laughing my head off. It was funny until my mother grabbed me and gave me a fine whooping on the side of the road, in the pouring rain. She beat me until she was tired; she beat me until her arms hurt, and she beat me until she got out all the anger and frustration and hatred for my father out of her system. A child can never understand why a mother would beat them for laughing – but she later apologized. As a grown woman today, I realize that if I was the source of release and relief for all that my mother was going through at that time, then I would gladly take that beating all over again. She was a strong woman. I never saw her cry, although I am sure she did, and as a mother of one child today, who has the help of a very good husband, I cannot even begin to imagine all that my mother endured as a single mother of four.

You see, growing up less fortunate and underprivileged can leave one feeling dumped – dumped into a poor, dysfunctional family, dumped into a volatile neighbourhood, dumped into life. People take our slow start and use it to mark us, practicing classism, which dictates how we treat people. People are treated based on where they come from and what they can afford, and not by the measure of their characters. But with all that dumping and burying, we come to learn that we are seeds, and a seed must be buried so it can bloom.

Chapter 2

Rebel Without a Cause

L et's put it this way; I was the life of the party. I laughed the loudest, played the hardest, and lived the liveliest. I was your typical girl next door. By the time I got comfortable in high school, I was a social butterfly. I was extremely confident, far from shy, and considered myself quite extroverted. I loved to initiate conversations, to engage with people, and by extension, give of myself. In hindsight, I have learned that being this way can be quite exhausting, but that is the way I believe God made me.

My first experiences at high school were a culture shock. I was now sitting and standing next to girls who otherwise I would never mingle with – Indians and Chinese, with hair so long and straight that it amazed me. Girls from all walks of life came to the school, and it excited me to be there. The school had a swimming pool, and we would take swimming as Physical Education. There was also a lovely tennis court that we could use anytime. What? Someone please pinch me! For someone like me, who had never been exposed to any of that stuff, I was in Heaven. And so, school became my haven. We had a huge group of trees at the entrance of the school, which provided shade for some concrete benches. This area was called 'the tree of parliament,' as this was where the girls congregated and chatted with their friends in their free sessions. I loved it. I had never seen girls sit so studiously, talking and laughing about any and everything. I was used to a more vulgar type, shouting and screaming, and I was truly happy to dwell among them. As a result, I was extremely sociable and got to know everyone. I was friends with the nerds, with the beauticians, the weirdos, the popular girls, and the in-betweens. School was my get away from my less than comfortable life at home.

Back at home, my older sister had moved out and had a baby. She was in an abusive relationship with her boyfriend at the time, and that really took a toll on my mother, which, in turn, took a toll on me. My eighteen-year-old brother had decided he wouldn't put up with my mother's ways either, so he subsequently moved out as well. All that was left were me and my younger sister, which is how it had always been, but now it felt lonelier, as though there was no one else to look to, it was all us.

I tried to become a tower of strength for my little sister. I wanted to shield her from some of the things I believed she was still too young to know, all the while struggling with my own self-identity. I began living a double life; at school I was this confident girl who was happy and carefree, laughing and smiling all day. But as soon as I touched the gate to enter our yard, all smiles were gone, and a sort of depression began to sink in. The days and nights were tumultuous. We shared yard space with a family that was extremely obnoxious. The woman was spiteful and would do things like light a fire whenever our clothes were on the line, play loud music at odd hours of the night, to which my mother's response was to turn up her own radio even louder. As a result, you had two people making unnecessary noise just to spite the other. My head is pounding as I remember this, as if I can hear the noise all over again in my head. Not to mention the countless quarrels between them; it was a nightmare, and it began to really affect me, although I didn't know it at the time.

While my mother did everything in her power to provide for us, sometimes the ends were not quite met, and we would go to bed with hot water sweetened with sugar for our supper or have some boiled dumplings with butter for dinner.

One Christmas day, my sister and I were left alone at home, as my mother was working, and we had corned beef sandwiches for dinner. That memory stayed with me because it was one of the saddest, loneliest Christmases I had ever had. Although my mother worked tirelessly to put food on the table, we still had many hungry days and nights because our father was nowhere to be found. He came around every once in a while, and whatever he brought was never enough to properly sustain us. As I grew older, I watched him come and go – never staying for more than five minutes, ignoring our phone calls most of the time. As my love for my father slowly drained from me, the bitterness slowly took its place. You see, what I didn't know then was:

When my father and my mother forsake me, then the LORD *will take me up. (Psalm 27:10).*

That meant my earthly father was not my sustainer or my provider. Yes, God did intend for him to play his role as a father and take care of his children, but even if he didn't, our Heavenly Father will still be there to pick up the slack.

So many of us carry feelings of neglect and abandonment throughout the course of our lives. If you are like me, you find yourself bringing up the tale of how your father left you or your mother left you – even when no one has asked, telling yourself that is why you are the way you are. When you hurt people or do things that are unseemly, you put on the never-ending tape of how you were abandoned, dancing to the only song on the playlist of your one-man pity party. The truth is, it is a one-man party. No matter how many friends or loved ones we think we have, no one likes to stick around at a pity party. But playing the victim can make us feel good, give us the attention we didn't get as children from those who should have given it to us. But we find out that God doesn't encourage this sort of victimized behavior either. He tells us so many times in His Word that we have the victory – we are victorious through Jesus Christ (See 1 Corinthians 15:57). When we don't know the life-changing words of the One who created us, we suffer, sometimes unnecessarily.

Have you ever heard the popular saying, if you don't stand for something, you will fall for anything? Similar to that, if you don't know God's truth about you, you will believe anything. Children's first example of love is what they receive from those set above them; now can you imagine what happens when all you have received is neglect? We don't know it at the time, but our minds bury this in a place so deep that even when we are married with children, we are still haunted by that grave. Those feelings must be uprooted like the weeds that torment a beautiful garden.

I didn't know all this then, so I changed. I began to hate authority, and then this fixation with being independent and my own boss was born. What I didn't know at the time is that God's natural law is that the man is the head of the household. So, whenever we have any kind of hurt or pain suffered at the hands of a man, the devil finds a portal to our hearts and our minds and begins to plant seeds of doubt, fear, and a whole lot of lies. Lies like *I don't need a man, I can and will become successful on my own*, or the one that is so popular nowadays, *Miss Independent*. 1 Timothy 2:11 tells us that a woman should learn quietly with all submissiveness. Well, if the head of the household has abandoned the household, then there is no man to learn from, and women had to learn to teach themselves and to keep their children going and the family afloat. What is amazing about this is that the devil thought he had won when he led our men astray, but what we didn't know is that:

"...all things work together for good to them that love God, to them who are the called according to His purpose. (Romans 8:28).

God always has a backup plan and we will see this plan unravel as our lives progress.

Child Abuse or Another Lie?

Rejection of authority and correction is just one of the result of children whose lives the enemy managed to set a foot in. I saw it with my older siblings leaving the home as soon as they were legally allowed to, and I saw it in myself very early on. Whenever I was corrected or beaten by my mother, this enormous amount of hatred for her would overtake me, and I wouldn't know where it came from or what to do about it. I wrote in my journals how much I hated her, and I made plans how I would run away the first chance I got. Then the times came when I did run away. There weren't many places to go, but my grandmother's house seemed good at the time. My mother would come and find me wherever I went and give me a fine spanking for what I did, and although no one likes a good whooping, knowing that would be the result of my disobedience made me think twice about running away again or disrespecting my mother in any way. If you look closely at where the world is today, corporal punishment – which is the act of spanking your child due to misbehaviour by that child – is illegal in a large majority of the world and growing. As a result, parents or teachers can be charged or imprisoned by the government for putting a hand on a child to correct behaviours deemed rude or disrespectful. It does not take a genius to see that this system is another of the enemy's way to pervert and go against everything that God says and has set in place to have a world that is good and running in harmony. Proverbs 13:24 tells us that:

*He that spareth his rod hateth his son:
but he that loveth him chasteneth him betimes.*

God clearly sets out guidelines for us to follow in every aspect of our lives, even in how to raise children, but as you can see in society today, there are oppositions and laws everywhere to ensure that we go against the word of God, and in return, raise children who go unpunished and therefore never learn from their mistakes.

A rebel is defined as a person who rises in opposition against an established leader. It's safe to say that that established leader was not only my mother but every system in my life that was set up to tell me no or otherwise. One way I thought I could rebel was choosing to have sex at the age of sixteen. I always grew up hearing that we shouldn't have sex until we are married, and I thought blah blah blah, who's going to stop me? I remember my poor boyfriend at the time wasn't even ready and seemed really scared, but miss bossy coaxed him into it. There was really no other reason that I wanted to do it, except that I had been told all my life that if I ever did so, 'this and that' would be my reward, and it was a challenge I was ready to take on. At the end of all the sweating and failed attempts, we finally managed to attain something similar to penetration, and when it was all over, I felt icky and disgusted. I wished I hadn't done it, and I couldn't understand what all the hype was over this 'sex thing.' But that was it, I had let the cat out of the bag, and my virginity was gone forever, just like that.

Grace Is Really Amazing

There is something about doing what we know is wrong. The build-up and the suspense can be enthralling, but at the end, you are left with this feeling of 'what did I just do?' We wish we could rewind time and take it all back. But we can't, and what we are left with is an open portal for worst to come. After feeling awful after that first encounter, I continued to do the 'sex thing' and engage in other activities that literally left my skin crawling every time I remember. Sexual immorality is one of the most common sins I believe that young adolescents suffer from. It is a time in our lives that we believe we know ourselves and we know what we want. We think we can face any consequence our actions bring on, and we block our minds from anyone who tries to tell us otherwise.

One day, my girlfriends and I decided to go to a music studio to "link up" with one of my friend's artiste friends. As I entered the dimly lit room filled with the essence of smoke and sex, I knew I was in a place that I didn't belong. But I was already there and couldn't afford to look like a coward and turn back, so I stuck it out. Naturally, the artiste friend had a few friends of his own, whose jobs I believe were to keep us busy while he kept my friend busy. The good thing about that time was that I still had a little resilience in me, and so I was not about to let those guys touch me in places only I should touch. They quickly saw that I was a hard nut to crack and went off to explore the more susceptible grounds of my other friends. I sat in that dark, musty studio and listened as my friends did things with complete strangers that children our age should not even know about doing. Looking back now, so many things could have gone terribly wrong that day. As naïve as I was to think that it was my serious face or badass personality that kept me untouched, it was the sheer grace of God that was upon my life that day. Otherwise, if those men had insisted that they were going to have a piece of me by will or by force, there was nothing I could have done about it, with them being bigger and stronger than I was. You see, the Bible tells us in Ephesians 2:8-9:

For by grace are ye saved through faith;
and that not of yourselves: it is the gift of God:
Not of works, lest any man should boast.

How many times have you gotten yourself into a situation that was way more than you had bargained for, and by the time you realize the mess you are in, it is far too late to do anything about it? That is what the grace of God is; Grace is God choosing to bless us rather than curse us as our sin deserves. It is God giving us the good that we do not deserve and keeping away from us all the bad that we have worked for.

I was still too foolish to know at that time that it was not my screw face or my 'works' that had saved me from being another victim of rape that day, the same way it is not what you have done for yourself that has kept you thus far. When the Lord tells us that His grace is sufficient for us, He is saying that there is nothing you can do that will cause His help and love for you to run out. There is nothing you can ever go through that will be too much for Him to handle in your life. All you have done and said that would cause anyone else to turn their backs on you and to be weary of you, none of that phases God. He is the burden-bearer who asks us to cast our cares on Him. But if you are a rebel like I was, that's not where your head is. Unfortunately, like me, you might not even know this. Did you even know that there is somebody who loves you so desperately that there is nothing you could possibly do to chase Him away? How could we know this? And even if you have heard this before, it is hard to believe because all we have seen in our lives show us people who give up on us because of the first mistake we make.

Today, we live in a world where most people are bleeding so badly on the inside that for them to feel any sort of acceptance for themselves is to reject someone else. Their life's mission is to make others feel inferior, so they can convince themselves that they are superior, a cut above the rest. Because this has become a societal norm, we hurt before we can get hurt. We no longer celebrate anyone else's success because we see that as us not being successful or lagging behind. We have learned to see ourselves through the dirty lens that others look at us through. If truth be told, we have done some dirty things to deserve that sort of treatment. We have not been as innocent and kind as we would like to think, and as a result, the treatment we are getting from those who know us is probably well-deserved, right? Wrong! As much of a rebel as we are, God is more of a rebel than we could ever be. That is the very essence of grace. That is why the devil was completely bowled over in shock, I believe, when Jesus came to earth to die for the redemption of our sins. Can you believe it? God, who is the epitome of holiness and righteousness, took the lowliest form – the form of man – who had all sinned and come short of His glory (See Romans 3:23) and died a gruesome death just to reunite our souls with Him. As rebellious as you think you are, my friend, our Father in Heaven is the most rebellious of all. He decided that He made you in His image and likeness, and no matter how much you run away from Him, He is not willing to let you go so easily. There is a popular song by the famous Jamaican artiste Jimmy Cliff, called "The Rebel in You," whose lyrics state that "if the rebel in me can touch the rebel in you, and the rebel in you can touch the rebel in me, then the rebels we be is gonna set us free." I believe Sir Jimmy had the same idea that God had from day one, because nothing, absolutely nothing:

For I am persuaded, that neither death, nor life, nor angels, nor principalities, nor powers, nor things present, nor things to come, nor height, nor depth, nor any other creature, shall be able to separate us from the love of God, which is in Christ Jesus our Lord. (Romans 8:38–39).

Now isn't that amazing!

Chapter 3

GOD DOESN'T CALL THE QUALIFIED

Shortly after my encounter at the studio, my half-brother met the Lord Jesus, and he was so excited about his new life and his newfound church family that he began taking my sister and me to church with him. It was the first in a long time that I had been to church, and I felt like an outcast in the beginning. It was an apostolic church where it was believed that the women should not wear pants, because it was 'men's clothing,' and they were not to wear jewellery or anything but their natural hair. I would show up in my jeans and earrings with my well-permed hair in some style or another, and you could tell with just one look that I didn't really fit in. But soon after being there, the stares and whispers from some of the members started to fade, and the words that were being preached from the pulpit started to pierce me. It wasn't so much about the teachings of hell and what will happen to us if we never come to accept God, but the teachings about His love, kindness, and mercy drew me in. Whenever the church sang songs and worshipped God, I looked around at the people with their eyes closed, hands thrown up in the air, heads flung back, and tears streaming down their faces, and I wondered what on earth they were experiencing. Why were grown people bawling like that? The air would feel so tense, as though you could cut the atmosphere with a knife. But I was always too concerned about how funny I would look with my hands in the air or crying. No, I did not want to look as ridiculous as they did. Those were the thoughts that encompassed me, yet I couldn't shake the feeling of try it and see. Something said to me, "Close your eyes, mouth the words of the song, and just try it and see." Well, I did it, and before you know it, my eyes were flung open again, and I was looking around to see if anyone was looking at me. Sure enough, no one cared. They were too busy fighting their own internal struggle the same way I was.

There is just something about the presence of God. I didn't know it at the time, but in God's presence, there is fullness of joy, and at His right hand, there are pleasures forevermore. It was the beginning of Him showing me the path of life (See Psalm 16:11). So, whenever I closed my eyes, it was as though I had stepped into another realm, one I had never experienced before or even knew existed. I was in His presence, and it felt like I had escaped my present world and there was no more time or thought of anything. There was no more worry or pain or anything – there was only a filling. I felt like I had become an empty glass, and someone was holding a giant jug over me, and that person was pouring something into me, and they poured and poured until I was running over, and it felt absolutely amazing. That was the beginning of my transformation, the beginning of His calling. I am sure now that He was always with me from my birth up until that moment, but on that day, I felt like it was my time now, and I could not shake the feeling. I would leave the church, the building, but I couldn't escape His presence. I felt like I had opened a door and no matter how much I tried to close it, it was always slightly ajar.

Joy Comes In The Morning

At home, things were the same. My mother still worked hard, day and night to support my sister and me. On the days that my mother did double shifts as a Security Officer to make ends meet, my sister and I would sit on the veranda bored out of our minds. We would talk about our dreams and desires of what we were going to do when we grew up and had our own money. When our mouths got tired, we would just sit there watching people go by. On most of those days, our empty fridge was the norm. We had figured out that the trick to getting our father to answer our phone calls, a.k.a. cry for food, was to block our caller ID so he wouldn't know it was us calling. Those private calls would catch him off-guard, and he would answer the phone with a strong, "Hello." Depending on whose turn it was, my sister and I knew we had only a matter of seconds to get our words in. We would say something like, "Daddy we're hungry. Can you bring food for us please?" His response was almost always, "Where is your mother?" as though her being home or not was a decisive factor in whether or not he would come. Those phone calls almost always ended in him telling us that he was on his way, but he only came an average of three out of ten times. Those days were so depressing, evening after endless evening we would sit on the veranda watching the sun go down, drowning in our sorrows, not knowing if those days would ever come to an end. You see, friend, those days must be experienced, but they are not here to stay.

What is your depressing factor? What dark cloud is looming over your head or your life in this present moment? It is there so that it can pass – it is not there to stay. I know it feels as though someone has stopped the pages in the book of your life on a bad chapter, but I promise you that is not the case. The less-than-desirable moments in our lives are hard to bear and painful to handle, almost like a cruel joke. However, they actually come to teach us a valuable lesson. Isn't it weird that something so saddening or unbearable can teach you a lesson and strengthen you?

The Word of God cannot lie, and do you know what it says? Job 23:10 states:

But he knoweth the way that I take:
when he hath tried me, I shall come forth as gold.

What does that mean to you? Well, I will tell you what it means to me; it means that God is allowing you to go through the trials you have experienced in the past or the one you are currently going through right now so that at the end of it, you will be a stronger, wiser, and more resilient you. Look at someone like Joyce Meyer, for example, who was abused sexually, physically, and emotionally by her father from the age of nine and was called a liar by her mother when she told her what was going on. She suffered in that situation for years until she was old enough to leave home. Today, she is one of the most famous Christian teachers and preachers and is known for her charismatic way of bringing the Word of God to millions of people through conferences, radio, and television shows and through her Hand of Hope ministry that travels around to the most desolate parts of the earth, helping as many poor people as they possibly can. Through her painful past, Joyce has been able to not only relate to the sufferings that so many of us endure, but she has also led so many persons, especially broken women who have likewise been abused, to the saving grace of Jesus Christ. In essence, through leading them to find Christ, she has led them to find themselves. I am of the opinion that Joyce could have never imagined on those days when her father painfully and forcibly took her innocence that she would be leading the life she does today. There are so many other persons like Joyce Meyers who have been through terrible situations in their past, who are now using that same story to free so many other people who are going through the same things. You need to know that your story will not end like this. God didn't promise that He would cause us to skip over the challenges in our lives, but He did promise that He will be with us every single step of the way. He said:

When thou passest through the waters, I will be with thee; and through the rivers, they shall not overflow thee: when thou walkest through the fire, thou shalt not be burned; neither shall the flame kindle upon thee. (Isaiah 43:2).

Notice that He didn't say 'pass over', He said *through*. What you are going through now, this thing that feels as though it is going to end you, is the thing that will birth you, the real you.

You may ask, *Why do I have to go through this? Why can't I discover myself or be able to help others without having to go through all this pain?* Well, would you want to go to a dentist who couldn't be bothered with the long arduous task of going to dental school to study for all those years, so he just bought his dental qualifications online? I'm sure not.

My brethren, count it all joy when ye fall into divers temptations; knowing this, that the trying of your faith worketh patience. (James 1:2-3).

You teach it better if you have lived it, and that, my friend, is exactly why God came down on this earth in the form of man, to teach us by example all that He requires from us when He calls us. He showed us that He is not a God who sits high and dictates what we should do but has no idea what it feels like to be human. So, what did He do? He came down as flesh, as His Son, Jesus Christ, so we can be confident that He is able to relate and that all He is telling us is indeed attainable.

When I decided to stop trying to close the door that had been opened by just a taste of God's presence, my biggest concern was that I would never be able to match up, to live up to the life of holiness and righteousness that was required. It seemed so unattainable, especially with my filthy mouth and lascivious ways. I was loud and aggressive, pushy and disrespectful. I thought, how could God love me? What could this spotless, righteous, almighty Being want with me? I thought surely I was the worst of them. I didn't know that all the things I didn't like, or thought was wrong about myself were exactly the things He wanted to use. For example, my big mouth, my confrontational and aggressive ways. He wanted the same qualities I had, minus the sin. In other words, He wanted me just as I am.

You are probably concerned about cleaning yourself up before you answer the Father's call. You tell yourself, "I'll do some more partying, get it out of my system first," or "I'll have to break up with my boy/girlfriend first so that I won't be tempted to have sex with them." Whatever excuses we give ourselves to try to buy time is completely unnecessary and is a complete waste of time. Because sin is an act that goes against God's law (See 1 John 3:4). James 1:14-15 says:

But every man is tempted, when he is drawn away of his own lust, and enticed. Then when lust hath conceived, it bringeth forth sin: and sin, when it is finished, bringeth forth death.

We will always be in the flesh, and the flesh is constantly lusting and tempted, so we need God's help – His Spirit – to clean up. We absolutely cannot do it on our own. So telling ourselves that we will come to God when we have made things right is just another way that the devil deceives us. You need His help to clean yourself up, so quit waiting on a day that will never come – where you clean yourself up to go to God, the only One who can clean you whiter than snow.

So where does that leave you? What am I supposed to do now, you might ask. Simple, stop trying to clean up or cover up your wrongdoings; confess them instead. Scriptures tell us that:

If we confess our sins, he is faithful and just to forgive us our sins, and to cleanse us from all unrighteousness. (1 John 1:9).

In Ezekiel 36:25, the Lord says:

Then will I sprinkle clean water upon you, and ye shall be clean: from all your filthiness, and from all your idols, will I cleanse you.

Don't sweat it. God specializes in calling the most unqualified of us all, and He wants you to come just as you are.

When I made the decision to get baptized, I would love to say it was because I had known all these amazing things and I had some glorious epiphany that made me willingly say, "Yes Lord, I'm ready!" That's probably how it happened for some people, but I was still oh so reluctant. I was afraid, to put it simply. I had no idea what was going to happen to me, and the life I was living had become comfortable for me. Change is scary, and a change into the unknown can be even more frightening. This is why so many of us take such a long time to say an official *Yes* to God. It's not because you don't believe in Him, and it's not because you don't feel His presence when you go into church. As a matter of fact, whenever you are in an atmosphere of worship and praise, the hairs on your arms and the back of your neck almost always stand erect, making every fibre of your being aware that a force much bigger and mightier than ever is among you. So, for some of you, it is not because you don't believe but because of fear. It is the same fear that prevents you from stepping out into the life you know you are to be living. It is the same fear that makes you procrastinate whenever you get ready to do that life-changing thing. Fear says you are not good enough even though everyone else is saying you can do it. Fear tells you to stay in that situation that is absolutely killing you, because it will be too hard out there on your own. Fear has an excuse for everything. But what is fear? Well, by definition, fear is an unpleasant emotion caused by the threat of danger, pain, or harm. Look back at some of the examples I listed above, and now think back on all the things you have ever wanted to do in your life, of all the changes you have dreamed of making, and see if you can pinpoint where in those changes the threat of danger is, where is the pain and the harm? Often there is no danger, no pain, yet we are so fearful. Doesn't this seem like deception? We are afraid but of what we do not know. After all is said and done, you will realize that unless there is a threat of danger, harm, or pain involved, the fear holding you hostage right now is an illusion – a false idea or belief – and the minute you can step outside of your mind and see this, then this non-existent belief called fear that has held you crippled and immobile for so long will free you immediately. However, you may want to argue further that the 'fear of the unknown' is a real thing. Answering God's call on your life doesn't have to be scary because though you may not know what you are getting yourself into, your Heavenly Father is omniscient; all-knowing. He is the Alpha and the Omega – the beginning and the end – and knows exactly what your future looks like. The way to overcome this fear is to trust God. He says:

For I know the thoughts that I think toward you, saith the Lord, thoughts of peace, and not of evil, to give you an expected end. (Jeremiah 29:11).

This is one promise you can hold on to as you consider making what will be the most important and most fulfilling decision of your life. Where there is a possible reason to fear, you still have no permission to do so. It is said that 'Fear not' or 'Do not be afraid' is mentioned in the Bible 365 times. Every single day we have a reason to be afraid, but whatever that reason may be, it is not an excuse to abort your dreams and desires. God implores us to have no fear, and He gives us a command for every single day of the year. Coincidence or not? Joshua1:9 says:

Have not I commanded thee? Be strong and of a good courage; be not afraid, neither be thou dismayed: for the Lord thy God is with thee whithersoever thou goest.

If I had known these things, I would have given my life to the Lord at a much younger age than I did. That decision gave me the tools I needed to start digging myself out of the pit that had been dug for me – the pit that was filled with hurt, rejection, depression, poverty, inferiority complex, low self-esteem, lack of confidence, sexual immorality, and so much more. Those are the things that stifle us, hoping that we will never make it out to discover the amazing life God has designed for us. When you make up your mind to take the plunge, to get baptized and say yes to all that God has in store for you, then you shall receive the shovel, the ladder, the rope, and all the necessary help you need to start climbing free from your pit of pain.

Chapter 4

He Qualifies the Called (Saved or Slaved?)

He held my hands, and I followed gingerly behind him, allowing him to lead me into the darkness. The night was almost pitch-black, as the moon was the only light and the bushes we stepped into scratched at my legs as I willingly followed this boy around one of the darkest corners I had ever seen.

We were on a large property in the countryside that was an old school campus, and the plot of land was big enough to cater to the large group of people that were there that week. The location was secluded enough to provide the kind of environment needed for a group of young people who were easily distracted to stay focused throughout the week. We came to a stop at a place behind a tall building where my dark prince felt was dark enough to do our dirty deed, a place where we would not be seen. My heart raced as I thought to myself, "This is it, no turning back now" while his mouth came down on my face hard and sloppy, not only lacking sight but experience too. My body shook in pleasure and regret as his fingers slipped up my skirt and began to fondle me, and we kissed and groped each other while leaning against the gritty, dirty wall of an old building. I pushed him away as I heard the footsteps and giggling of some of our peers, probably looking for us. I was sure they knew what we were up to, but as they were unable to find us in the darkness, I ran from around the corner acting as though I had been doing nothing wrong.

We joined the group of people who were there with us, the campsite where our church had set up lodgings for the week to host their Annual Youth Camp and continued to act like two innocent people. Looking back now, the fact that as children and young adults we can be so daring to do such a thing at a church camp is bewildering to me. We knew that kind of thing was completely off limits, and we knew that if we had gotten caught, it would be extremely embarrassing for us – for me at least – yet that didn't stop us. It makes me wonder what is wrong with us. How can we know that doing something wrong can be so damaging to our names and reputation and still take the risk?

My many escapades did not end there after giving my life to God. I continued to be a daredevil. As a matter of fact, after we left that campsite, my dark prince and I hooked up again, this time in the privacy of his home. He was a handsome boy who attended the same church I did, and although he was not baptized and wasn't an official member, he was at church every week and almost every day. He lived just a stone's throw away from the church and started going because of the influence of his grandmother. We were in his grandmother's house doing what the Lord must have cringed to watch. I knew better, and the sex part is not what I wanted initially. In the beginning, I meant well – don't we always?

I gave my life to Christ with all the good intentions of remaining pure and righteous for Him. But as I came to find out, good intentions are useless without the right knowledge and understanding of how things work. He was a great-looking guy, and I had a big crush on him. I knew he was the bad boy type because I had seen him around the church. He was slick and cool, getting the attention of all the girls. When he started to show an interest in me, in the most naïve way, I was honoured. Little did I know that he had just been around the block and was ready for a new adventure, one he had yet to unclothe.

After only a very short while of texting and talking over the phone, and our brief 'feel-up' in the country, I was now in his home having sex with him. Like most unfortunate situations, the sex was rushed, void of emotion or sensitivity, sweaty, icky, and a complete waste of time and good virtue. What do you think happened after that? Do you think I rode off into the sunset with my new boo and was now his doting girlfriend who he was so in love with and committed to? Of course not. Situations where we sell ourselves short and leave our standards and high morals at home almost always never end well. We are left used and abused and feeling like a cheap prostitute. At least, that was how I felt, and with the last shred of dignity that I could afford to muster up, I ignored him at church just as well as he ignored me. I walked past him with my head held high and my nose in the air. I thought to myself, *If you think I'm going to be pining after you and blowing up your phone wondering why you've stopped calling me, then you've got another thing coming.* But I was nothing but a silly girl because, although I have no proof, I'm almost certain that he just checked me off on his list of sex achievements, and he probably had a good boasting session with his friends about it too. Now they knew what I did, and as much as I would like to act like I was nice and proud, I was nothing but another slutty church girl who was quick to spread her legs. That's how I saw myself for a long while after that, and it was pretty much the beginning of a downward spiral.

Where Sin Abounds, Grace Abounds Even More

Shortly after my eighteenth birthday, my mother lost the job that she had held for over twenty years. Well, she hadn't completely lost it. Something had gone wrong at work, and she was placed on suspension until they could decide what to do with her position. That meant our already hard life and high debt was about to become harder and higher.

I was doing a short stint at a financial institution that summer, being lucky enough to have been selected as one of the young people to work for a little less than a month in order to gain work experience while earning. The institution I had been placed at was a far distance away, as it was located at one of our two international airports. There was only one bus that went there, and if I missed that bus, I was sure to be late.

I always tend to do my best with every new opportunity, and that is exactly what I did as I excitedly went to work each day. Not only did I love to work and push myself to my highest potential, but the income was well needed, and the job was a blessing, to say the least. My mom had not lost her job yet, but I knew that my paycheck would help me complete the final year of my associate degree before I moved on to University to do my bachelor's.

I went to work early every morning and quickly became a hit with most of the staff there, especially the men. By that time, however, I had told myself that men were like sharks. A new and pretty face was like fresh meat for them, and when they saw one, it was as though they smelled blood and would always move in for the kill. As a result, their attention did not faze me one bit, and I continued to do the work I was given while ignoring their unwanted advances. So, you can imagine my shock and dismay when after only a few short weeks, I got a call from the recruitment agency telling me that the person who oversaw the summer interns had asked that I not return the following week. They said I did not return to work on time whenever I left to cash my paycheck at the end of each week. Not only was that a lie, but it just did not make any sense. All the summer interns were given time to go and cash their paychecks, and I did not abuse my time. Also, if someone felt that I was abusing my time, why didn't they call me and warn me? I was devastated, to say the least.

I went home that weekend wondering what went wrong, and who would want me out of there so badly, and more importantly, why? Little did they know that the God of all grace had a purpose on my life, and no devil in hell was going to thwart that purpose. That same weekend, the administrator of the recruitment agency, who I will call Mrs. Brown for the sake of this story, called me at home.

The reason for my dismissal didn't make sense to her, and she said I should report to the Head Office on Monday morning for a transfer. As fate would have it, none of the other organizations had any space to accommodate me, either that or it was just too late to transfer me, and much to Mrs. Brown's disappointment, I had to be placed at the Head Office of the recruitment agency to complete my tenure. I was elated when I got the call, and I thanked God for another chance. But I was in for a shock as my week in a new place began. Was I imagining things or overthinking? I could be mistaken, but I was almost certain Mrs. Brown, who was in charge of placing us and had called me back to work at the Head Office seemed to dislike me very much. When I got to the head office, I noticed that I was the only high school student who was an intern there. They made it no secret that only University students worked at the Head Office. But before I could feel proud, Mrs. Brown and the other college interns made it their duty daily to remind me that I did not belong there. I had never felt so out of place and insignificant in my entire life. The place was lovely, with nice, clean offices in an upscale work environment and people on the corporate ladder climbing away. It was my dream to dress up and go to work in a fancy office, but at that moment, it was starting to feel like a nightmare. The place was fun and buzzing with things to do, yet I was never much a part of those things. No matter how much I tried to put my feelings aside and dive in, I was usually forced out of the fun just by the attitude of those I worked with. I could not understand it. I spent hours agonizing over questions like what did I ever do to these people? Why didn't Mrs. Brown like me? I work hard; whenever I finished a task, I didn't sit and waste time, I let them know so that they can give me more work. I was nice to them; I smiled, so why didn't they like me? One or two persons would speak to me if I said something to them, but there was an overall tension and unspoken words. I could not figure it out, and I eventually decided to leave it alone.

As the remaining weeks passed by, I stopped trying to fit in and kept to myself. Soon their dismissive treatment of me paled in comparison to my more urgent needs – a job. My mother was not working often, and my small stipend was helping to sustain us.

It was the final week of my summer employment, and I was worried about what would happen to us afterwards. It hit me like a ton of bricks that I was not going to be able to go back to my final year of sixth form. I needed to work so I could help my mother support us. Besides, I was tired of going to school with little to no lunch money anyway, and having my own money seemed like the best thing to me. There was only one problem – where would I get a job on such a short notice? I had only a week until the summer job was done, then school would start in only a matter of days. I was only a high school graduate at that time, I did not have much qualification or experience to get the nice job that I had in my mind. I told my mother I was willing to get a job in KFC or any fast-food restaurant, and I would clean the toilets if I had to. What was important to me was working while I sent myself back to school.

The last day of work came, and as my unlucky fate would have it – or so I thought – my mother had no money to give me to go to work that day. All she had was one hundred Jamaican dollars, and that was only enough to pay for a taxi one way. Proving to be the strong, resilient person she has been my entire life, she did not encourage me to sit at home and have a pity party. She could have said, "Ok, my love, it's the last day of work, and you have no bus fare or lunch money, so sit this one out; they will understand." Instead, she came up with a plan. She said, "Take this one-hundred-dollar bill and keep it for your bus fare to get back home. Wake up early in the morning before the sun rises and walk to work. If you do this before the sun is fully out, the walk won't be hot and sweaty. Then when it's lunchtime, and you get hungry, make yourself a cup of tea so that you won't get gassy. In the evening, you take that money and take a bus home." I had to do what my mother said, and boy was I glad I did. That final day of work, when I had no money to buy breakfast or lunch, and I was obedient enough to walk to work, was the day that my life shifted on its axle and purpose sprung forth in the most amazing way ever.

I had to wake up and walk to work before the sun dawned and its blazing rays touched the earth, so I got to work on the very last day two hours early, arriving before everyone but the Security Guard. I made myself a cup of tea and sat down to enjoy the quiet tranquillity of the empty office. As I took in my surroundings, I reflected on my days there, and I believe I was feeling a sense of nostalgia. Despite everything that had happened there, I had really enjoyed the experience and was grateful for the opportunity. As my mind went back to what was next for me, and the job-hunting that was to come, the phone rang. I thought to myself, *Who could be calling so early at 7 a.m., when the offices open at 9?* As the ringing shrilled out into the empty office, I ran to answer it; after all, I was the only one there.

"Hello, good morning." I answered.

The words that followed were life-changing. "Good morning," responded the gentle voice on the other side of the phone, "May I speak with Mrs. Brown?"

"I'm sorry, she is not here yet. May I take a message for her?" I asked.

She told me her name, where she was calling from, and then she told me to tell Mrs. Brown that she was looking for a bright, young person who was not going back to school to come and work for a well-known company. I could not believe the words that were coming out of her mouth. It took my brain about two seconds to process what she said before I practically shouted at the woman, "I'm a bright young person not going back to school!"

"Ok great," She responded, "Send me your resume."

I grabbed a pen and paper and wrote down the email address that she provided, and as I hung up the phone, I could not believe what had just happened.

As I quickly retrieved my resume and sent it to her, something told me not to mention a word of it to Mrs. Brown or the other interns when they got in. If I did, it would no longer be my resume that they would be reviewing, and I kept my good fortune under tight wraps. Understandably, I was no longer hungry and would not be for the rest of the day. My stomach was filled with joy.

That fateful Friday I sent my resume off and was invited to go to the company for an interview the following Monday. The interview was a success, and on Tuesday I was told I would begin work that Friday. It had taken me one day of obedience but took God one phone call to move me out of a finished summer job into a job at one of the largest global companies in the country in a matter of one week. With no work done on my part, but a little prayer and one act of obedience and faith, God changed my life forever. Seven years later, I am still working for that company today, growing from strength to strength, and experiencing new mercies and favor every single day.

I shared that because I need you to understand that where sin abounds, grace abounds even more (See Romans 5:20). God is not moved or daunted by how much wrong you have done or by how heavy your sins measure on the non-existent 'sin-scale.' His grace is sufficient for you. It warms my heart every single day to know that on my best days when God does something amazing that often moves me to tears of joy, it is the same God who looked ahead in time and saw that I was going to do something wrong. Yet He chooses to still bless me today, despite what I do tomorrow.

He is not intimidated by your actions, it doesn't matter what you have done. He loves you today just as much as He did when you were a sweet, innocent baby who could do no wrong. Jesus came so that there would be an abundance of grace to lead you to a life of overcoming sin. I don't know how it works, but the more you do wrong, the more the grace of God will fill you with His love and acceptance. The more of His love you encounter, the less you will want to remain the same. God wants to move in your life in such a powerful way that there can be no denying that it is only Him. You will develop a desire to change and surrender your heart and life to Him completely.

God does not call the qualified, He qualifies the called. He doesn't need to use someone who has been a good Christian all their life. In fact, in an uncanny way, the Lord specializes in using people who are the best at being bad. Take Paul the apostle, for example, he was first called Saul and was known for his hatred and ardent persecution of Christians. He sought permission from the high priest to go to a place called Damascus to imprison more Christians there. However, on his way to Damascus, Paul had an encounter with Jesus. A bright light knocked him down and blinded him, and he heard the voice of Jesus speaking directly to him. The rest is history. That encounter with God led him to getting baptized, regaining his sight, and becoming one of the greatest apostles of all time. Now that's what I call *qualifying the called,* and just like Paul, God has called you by His grace.

He tells us in His Word:

*Before I formed thee in the belly I knew thee;
and before thou camest forth out of the womb
I sanctified thee, and I ordained thee a prophet
unto the nations. (Jeremiah 1:5).*

God finds great pleasure in using the most rebellious and least deserving of us all. When you begin to make use of the amazing privilege of prayer you have been given, God will reveal Himself to you more and more. You will feel completely unworthy in His presence, but you will find that there is not a judgment or admonishment of you, only pure love that will wash over you and fill you from the inside out. This feeling can be described as a fullness of joy. It is not about your track record of sin or how unqualified or unworthy you are to do the task God is calling you to do – it is about God's commitment to using weak people with deep flaws to do greater things than they could have ever imagined, and that includes you.

Chapter 5

Alternative Facts and Lies Disguised

A s you begin this new journey of healing and digging yourself free from the debris of pain that you have suffered in your life, you should know that some days you are going to feel completely broken and rejected. You may feel defeated, wondering why giving your life to God has not made you feel better yet. In fact, after the initial bliss has worn off, you may actually feel worse than you did before because now that you are no longer on the side of evil, you are now target practice for the devil, and he is going to come at you with every weapon he can find. But, not to worry, his tricks may be overwhelming to you, but is there anything too hard for the Lord? If you pay attention, you will soon learn that you wield a very powerful shield – the shield of faith – to block his fiery darts and avoid getting burned.

I do not want you to make the mistake of believing that coming to Christ will be the end of all your troubles and temptations. If you think that way, then you couldn't be more wrong. Your enemy, the devil, prowls around like a roaring lion, seeking someone to devour (See 1 Peter 5:8-9). He will try to mess with your mind by feeding you lies, and deception will be the name of the game. Allow me to help you understand some ways in which the devil will attempt to get into your head and feed you lies that can keep you in bondage, if you do not know that they are lies and if you don't have the proper tools to fight back.

Lie number one – Answering God's call on your life is the end of all trouble, and there will be no more struggles or wars to face. I know, I know, I wish this was true too. Who wants to know that they will be fighting for the rest of their life? Won't we get tired? The answers are probably no one and yes, we will. You are going to have trials and temptations, and quite frankly, it can be exhausting. God did not lie to us though. He told us plain and simple that in this world we will have trouble. There is a real battle going on, the fight between good and evil, and whether you like it or not, you are a part of that fight. Now that you have chosen to serve the Lord, you are no longer friends with the bad guys – nor were you ever – and closing your eyes and hoping all this 'bad stuff' will go away is all good and well, but, unfortunately, it won't change anything.

God will allow you to encounter trials and tribulations because they will build your character. We are called to rejoice in our sufferings, knowing that suffering produces endurance and endurance produces character, and character produces hope. You are called to count it all joy when you meet trials of various kinds, for the testing of your faith will produce perseverance; in the end, you will be perfect and complete, lacking nothing. The Lord told us, in this world we will have trouble, but He also promised us that we should take heart and be encouraged because He has overcome the world. In the end, God wins, and so will you. In the meantime, rejoice in hope, be patient in tribulation, and be consistent in your prayer life. It doesn't matter how long it takes, five minutes or two hours, pray without ceasing.

Lie number two – Those who hate you and are trying to slander your name and tear down your reputation should be gossiped about and hated in return; after all, they are the enemy and they started it first.

This is another popular lie. Everywhere you look today, you will find someone who is constantly slandering your name or just talking behind your back. Sometimes the reason they do this is completely unknown, and other times it is due to something that happened in the past. Maybe you need to offer an apology for something you have done or said in the past, but even if you don't, that gives them no right to treat you cruelly. However, in situations that create conflict and arguments, there is an invisible third party who loves to stay just that – invisible. If you keep fighting with your family or colleague without figuring out that this battle is not even between you and that person but is a result of a spiritual battle, you are in for a miserable time.

Ephesians 6:12 tells us that we wrestle not against flesh and blood but against principalities and powers and the rulers of the darkness in this world, against spiritual wickedness in high places. I wish my mom had known this on those days when our neighbour found new ways to torment us every day, whether by blasting her music at a deafening decibel or by lighting up a fire to smoke our clothes whenever we did our laundry. I wish I had known this when I fired back at every mean thing someone said to me or behind my back. I would not have wasted my time confronting those persons, which resulted in more conflicts and opening up of wounds, and neither would my mother. Instead of 'clapping back' at every mean thing said or getting even over every mean thing done, we could have fought back the right way, the effective way, on our knees in prayer.

Instead of confronting people in the natural, you must confront the spirits working through them. That is what the Bible meant when it said we do not fight against flesh and blood. We fight against spiritual wickedness in high places. In order to wage an effective fight, we too must employ our spiritual soldiers in high places. You must pray and ask God to fight those battles for you, to send His angels forth and to arrest the evil spirits that are working through our brothers and sisters, and to replace the evil with His spirit of love and grace. It won't be easy, but the quicker you start practicing this, the more positive results you will see. Think about it – if you continue fighting against your supposed enemy in the physical, you are left unhappy after confronting that individual and so are they. No one wins, and no one is left smiling but the devil.

The Bible tells us that the weapons of our warfare are not carnal (See 2 Corinthians 10:4). You don't bring a knife to a gun war. Put on the whole armour of God so you will be able to stand against the enemy's tricks. Salvation is your helmet, righteousness is your breastplate, your waist wears the belt of truth, your shoes are prepared with the readiness to announce and declare the goods news of peace, faith is your shield, and the Word of God is your sword. Use these tools while praying to God for His help and never give up.

Lie number three – Getting hurt and/or rejected by church people means that church is not right for you, and it's best to just watch a sermon from home or even worse, skip church altogether. First, you need to know that you are not saved by going to church – you become saved by faith when you believe in the Lord Jesus Christ and that He died for the redemption of your sins. You repent of your sins and are baptized in His name (See Romans 10:9–10 and John 3:5). Also, as a Christian, you will come to know that the church is not the edifice, but it is the people who worship there that make up the church. This edifice, however, is the place where the church can come together and worship God in one accord. Among the church, you can and will find a family who you can look up to, get good advice from, be there in times of need, help and teach you how to grow in your faith, and you will find a place where you feel like you belong. Unfortunately, the people among whom you should be able to find trust and acceptance will often let you down in many ways.

This lie is a tricky one because each person's situation is different and what one person is experiencing may be vile while others may be a matter of misunderstanding or miscommunication. As a result, a solution that is right for one person may not be right for another. However, if you consider yourself to be a follower of Christ and your church attendance has fallen drastically, it's time to ask yourself, *What does God our Father say about this?* After all, you don't stop going to the doctor because sick people are there, do you? Do you stop going to the gym because fat people go there? So why do we allow the devil to convince us that too many hypocrites go to church, so it's best we don't go?

I have seen many people get offended by someone's response to them or lack thereof, and their first response is to stop going to the place of worship. I used to fall for this lie too. But it hit me that if a nurse in a hospital disrespects me, I might report her to her superiors, but I surely won't get up and walk out of that hospital. The hospital has what we need. It has the medicine to make us get well and feel better, and we tell our self that no one is going to let us walk away from what we need. We should look at going to church the same way. Here are some reasons why going to church is extremely important and should not be neglected:

- Fellowship with the brethren acts as evidence that you are walking in the light.

But if we walk in the light, as he is in the light, we have fellowship one with another, and the blood of Jesus Christ his Son cleanseth us from all sin. (1 John 1:7).

You will find that you are sometimes dabbling in darkness, but continuously attending church will surely help you get back on the straight and narrow; it will get you *lit* again.

- When you attend church, you receive revelations about God's Word that edify and free you. You receive deliverance because in the church you will find people with different spiritual gifts, such as healing, deliverance, prophecy, word of knowledge, and so on. God will put the keys to unlock your life's blessing in the hands of another person, and in order to unlock this blessing, you first must come in contact with that person.

- It was Christ's habit to go into the synagogue to worship God and to teach. If Christ went to teach, why should we not go to learn? If He went to worship, shouldn't we follow His example by attending church? (See Luke 4:16, Mark 1:21). As a follower of Christ – though we won't always get it right – we should aim to do just that, follow Christ.

Lie number four – If tragedy takes you or someone you love, it is because of something bad you have done, and God is punishing you. This is one of the most popular lies. Let's explore it at different angles and discover the truth behind it:

- For so long, I personally suffered because of this one. Every move I made to try to become a better person, the devil was there behind me whispering in my ear, reminding me of my past and all the less-than-pleasant things I had done, and sometimes still did. I was, and still am, far from perfect, and the devil made sure I never forgot it. This lie held me down for so long. Have you ever been in class and the teacher asked a question that no one else knew the answer to, but you did? As much as you were sure you had the answer, something kept telling you not to raise your hand. If you did, you would quickly put it down. Then the teacher, clearly disappointed that no one knew this answer, would reveal it, and you beat yourself up for not having given it a try. Call it fear, low self-esteem, or lack of confidence – there are plenty of ways to dress it up. But it all comes down to us not being sure of who we are, what we know and what we can bring to the table, and to be sure, you first have to know. For a lack of knowledge, the people perish, my friend (See Hosea 4:6), and so it is important to find out the truth of what God says about you. It wasn't until I came across a particular verse that truth hit me in the face like a ton of bricks, and I held onto it like the anchor that it was until I was free from the ocean of lies that threatened to end me. Romans 8 came to me at a time when I really needed to know that no matter what I had done, no matter how dirty I thought my past was, there was absolutely no criticism or disgust on God's part. I was justified by His righteousness and am now righteous because He is. It is the same for you. Do not let any devil in hell cause you to continuously walk in shame over anything you have done, for:

There is therefore now no condemnation to them which are in Christ Jesus, who walk not after the flesh, but after the Spirit. (Romans 8:1).

It gets even better as you read further.

- The book of Job speaks of a man who loved God very much and he tried hard to be a righteous man. The devil saw this and wanted to put Job to the test, telling God that Job was only righteous because of how much God blessed him. If God should take away Job's blessings, then Job would curse God. So, God obliges the devil and allows him to put Job to the test. He could do anything he wanted to him, except kill Job. After losing all his children and wealth and being struck with an awful disease, Job cries out to God in Job 7:20:

I have sinned; what shall I do unto thee, O thou preserver of men? why hast thou set me as a mark against thee, so that I am a burden to myself?

He wanted to know what he had done to deserve what was happening to him.

The truth is, we live in a fallen world overridden with sin, and as a result, bad things happen every day. People always want to know why bad things happen to good people. Sometimes we can find what we believe to be answers from stories in the Bible, for example, the book of Job. Although Job did not know it, he hadn't done anything bad to deserve all he was going through, but God allowed it to prove to the devil that Job's righteousness was not because of all He had given to Job. The Lord answered Job, asking him:

Where wast thou when I laid the foundations of the earth? declare, if thou hast understanding. (Job 38:4)

God is not obligated to give us all the answers we seek, but that is where trust comes in. Will you trust Him enough to know that whatever you are going through, whatever you went through, and whatever is to come has a higher purpose? Will you stay faithful and, like Job, refuse to curse God? Though Job went through a tumultuous time, he remained faithful to the Lord, and God restored Job's prosperity and doubled his possessions.

- Finally, the good book tells us that the Lord chastens those He loves and scourges everyone who He receives as His son (See Hebrews 12:6–7). What does this mean to you? To chasten someone, by definition, is to correct him or her, often with the use of some pretty steep punishment. Chasten is related to the word 'chastise,' which means to punish severely, and both words can be traced back to the Latin root *'castus,'* which means morally pure. To scourge means to whip someone as punishment. Therefore, there will be times when you will experience a phase in your life where God shuts certain doors and blocks you from things you may desire. It will be painful as though a parent is disciplining you, and like all children being punished, you won't like it one bit. Whatever His reason is for doing it, you can rejoice, knowing that God is chastening you because He loves you. What kind of son or daughter would you be if your Father left you to do things your own way, things that will hurt you or worse? If you have children of your own, you may know exactly what I am talking about. I have a daughter, and whenever she does something wrong, for example, go into the street to play without my permission or supervision, I discipline her because something out there could hurt her. I do this because I love her; otherwise, I would leave her to her ways and allow whatever may to happen to her. God is a good Father, and He will not sit idly by while you, His child, do things that will only hurt you.

Lie number five – You don't need to pray to receive the Holy Spirit. After you have been baptized in water, it is imperative for you to be baptized of the Spirit. The Holy Spirit came when Jesus Christ rose from the dead and ascended into Heaven. The Holy Spirit is a part of the Trinity of the Godhead and is your comforter. Christ said it Himself in John 14:16–17:

And I will pray the Father, and he shall give you another Comforter, that he may abide with you forever; Even the Spirit of truth; whom the world cannot receive, because it seeth him not, neither knoweth him: but ye know him; for he dwelleth with you, and shall be in you.

With the oppression in today's world and the persecution that you will suffer if you refuse to do things that are immoral or illegal, you will need all the comfort you can get. Not only that, it is the Holy Spirit who will know what to pray when you don't have the words to pray for yourself. There will be times when all you can do is groan, and the Holy Spirit within you will cry out on your behalf, speaking directly to God in other languages called tongues:

Likewise the Spirit also helpeth our infirmities: for we know not what we should pray for as we ought: but the Spirit itself maketh intercession for us with groanings which cannot be uttered. (Romans 8:26).

I implore you to do further research on the Holy Spirit and who He is, because He is one Being you don't want to live without.

Lie number six –Tithing is not necessary and is a thing of the past. On the issue of tithing, one couldn't have found a bigger sceptic than me. For the most part, I hated to hear anything about giving money, as I was struggling financially and could not pay my monthly bills comfortably. I was being so badly compensated that my salary would run out on my bills. That meant unpaid bills, no money for food or bus fare for work, and least of all, no money for leisure. As a result, whenever I heard anyone preach or teach about giving in church, my soul would be grieved. I would get so upset that I would be ready to get up and leave church. No matter how awesome the sermon was, if the preacher ended the service with a call to give, it would spoil things for me. Just thinking back on this, I cannot believe how lost I was. I was so deceived. Can you imagine how much the devil stole from me the longer I held on to this lie?

There are so many times in the Bible where God tells us to give, and what we will receive if we do give. But I had spent so many years hearing the negative remarks that others made around me, for example, pastors only take our money to buy a big house and car for themselves. I didn't understand that even if some pastors were misusing church funds, it was not my place to use that as an excuse not to give. I was sinning as well by disobeying the Word of God, the command of God. I am so grateful that God is such a faithful and patient Father. When He sees us as lost as I was, with the terrible thoughts I had, instead of giving up on me, He took His time and taught me the truth that it was not my concern what the pastors did with the money. My responsibility is to obey His commands.

When God asks us to give to Him a tenth of all our earnings, it is surely not because the God who created this world, this universe, has any use for our money. He took His time and taught me that giving was not for Him, but for me. He taught me how to trust Him and to believe that it is He who sustains me and not my job.

Sometimes God will use whatever medium He has to erase the lies we have held on to for so long and replace them with the truth. For me, it was when my husband came into my life. He truly believed in worshipping God in spirit and in truth, and that meant obedience to all aspects of His Word, including tithing. I would argue with him and ask him how I could give out of what I don't have? He showed me that I put aside my rent and other bills first; instead, I should put aside my tithe first. And wherever the money ended, I would have to trust God to make a way. It was hard for me to do at first because all

I could think about was my utilities getting cut off and the landlord knocking at the door. Those concerns finally convinced me that I was not fully surrendered to God – I didn't trust Him as much as I should. I must say that I have proven God time and time again. God cannot lie – He just can't. Ever since I decided to change my thinking and put God first by giving Him what belongs to Him and owe everyone else, the blessings have been amazing, and the peace I experience is invaluable. Never have I seen miracles such as what tithing and giving have shown me. How can it not be a miracle to go from always being broke before all the bills are paid to having bills paid and surplus after tithing?

Give, and it shall be given unto you; good measure,
pressed down, and shaken together, and running over,
shall men give into your bosom. For with the same
measure that ye mete withal it shall be measured
to you again. (Luke 6:38).

God says to prove Him *now* (See Malachi 3:8–12). If you know anything about God, His Word means everything. He exalts His Word over His own name (See Psalm 138:2). God is the original man of His Word, and you can count on it. His Word is His bond.

My friend, you can't fight or have any chance of winning a war you don't know you are fighting in. You cannot pass a test that you have not studied for. Knowledge is power. We hear this all the time, but do we really believe it? Ask yourself what these words really mean. God said it Himself, "My people perish for a lack of knowledge."

I implore you, begin to seek knowledge; uncover the truth about the lies you don't even know you have been told, and may still be believing. This book you are holding in your hands is a great first step toward that, but the book that has all truth, the Holy Book, holds the keys that will unlock everything you have ever desired. It holds the map that nomads like us need in an ever-changing world. Try to let it become your best friend; I know I have.

Chapter 6

Lover of Your Soul

Y ou will never experience a love more fulfilling and complete than the one you will experience with our Lord and Saviour Jesus Christ. I have never known another who could stimulate my mind, body, and soul the way He does. Some people know God the Father, the Protector, the Provider. Some know Him as the One who fights our battles and is strong and mighty. But do they know God the lover? Do you?

David, the famous king of the Bible who God called a man after His own heart, describes this love in the best way he knew how when he said:

*Because thy lovingkindness is better than life,
my lips shall praise thee. (Psalms 63:3).*

If you have ever wondered what real love feels like or if love really does exist, it does. If you have ever been parched in the love department or looked for love in all the wrong places, stop right now, because love has been looking for you.

There was this woman, though her name was never disclosed, but people tell her story all the time. She was called *the woman at the well* and you will find her story in John 4. She was from a place called Samaria, and at the time, people from Samaria had no dealings with Jews. This woman went to a well to draw water at a time of day when the sun would have been scorching hot, and it was not the custom of her people. They only went to draw water when the sun was low in the sky, in other words when the time was much cooler. Theologists and other Bible scholars say that this woman did this because she lived a dirty and shameful life, and it was highly likely that the people in her community berated her because of it. To avoid them, she went to draw water at a time when no one else would. Jesus knew all things and purposely went to the well at that time of day just to meet with the woman. The minute this woman came into the presence of the Lord, she knew something was different about this particular Man.

While the Lord was talking to her about water, she was taking it literally. Then He said to her:

If thou knewest the gift of God, and who it is that saith to thee, Give me to drink; thou wouldest have asked of him, and he would have given thee living water. (John 4:10)

And even then, the poor woman did not get it, as her response was:

Sir, thou hast nothing to draw with, and the well is deep: from whence then hast thou that living water? (John 4:11).

This is how clueless some of us are when we start to interact with the Lord. We have for so long been blinded by our ways, by what society thinks of us and how it expects us to act, that when we encounter change, we have no idea what it is. But, thankfully, the God we serve is patient and kind.

As Jesus spoke with the woman, He began to tell her all her business: She had had five husbands, and the man she was currently with was not her own. She had many sexual partners and either couldn't keep a man or didn't want to. She was possibly ostracized and was sleeping with a man who did not belong to her. But when she realized who she was dealing with, she was hit with a taste of what true satisfaction was.

God revealed Himself to her, and it is written that the woman left her bucket at the well, forgetting what her initial intent was, forgetting what the people she lived amongst thought of her, and ran to share the good news, telling people to come meet a man who told her everything about herself. I believe what caused the shift in that woman's mind was that, although this Man knew her deepest, darkest secrets, He still spoke and dealt with her with such love and tenderness that she did not feel chastised at all. Instead, she became empowered to the point where she no longer cared what anybody thought of her. All that mattered was Jesus and how He made her feel, and she wanted to share that with everyone. That is exactly what happened to me, and it will happen to you as well. It is impossible for you to encounter God and remain the same. A change must take place.

You may choose to go back to your old ways, but it does not mean you did not experience a life-changing encounter. You will find that no man or woman will ever be able to fill the God-sized hole that is in your heart. Some people use work, school, or their children as a distraction from the emptiness inside, and so you may find different things to busy yourself with. But ignoring it will simply not make it go away.

No Man Can Fill the God-Sized Hole in Your Soul

I was hit hard by this reality one day as I lay beside my husband after we made sweet love to each other. Yes, the sex was great, but as soon as those moments of blissful pleasure ended, I remember feeling so empty inside. I had this man who adored me and gave me whatever I wanted. He was faithful to me, treated me with respect, and most of all, I was truly in love with him, and I didn't have to force it or lie about my feelings. So why was I lying awake in the wee hours of the morning staring at the ceiling with tears running hot and fast down the sides of my face? Something was missing. I had this huge void inside me, and in that moment, it hit me. The beautiful man beside me would never be able to fill the void, and neither could I fill the hole that would be in his heart.

We all have that missing piece of the puzzle that gnaws at us, desperate to be filled. The more we try to stuff things into that empty spot, the deeper we will find our self falling into misery, depression, and unhappiness. Many people experience this inexplicable unhappiness. It is hard to define, and you just can't put your finger on what it is. To fill it, one might take up a new partner or a new hobby, anything to try to forget this void. I found out the hard way that the hole in my heart could not and will never be filled by anyone but the One who made that heart.

That night, when I laid in bed staring at my husband, willing him to wake up and comfort me, I knew I was being unfair to expect this man to fix something that he had no idea was broken and no clue how to fix. I was taken back to when I was just a young teenage girl. I saw myself sitting in a corner crying. I can't remember what I was so upset about, but it really had me feeling messed up. In that moment when I needed Him desperately, God came, just like He promised in His Word that He will never leave or forsake us. As I felt Him wrap His invisible, but so very tangible arms tightly around me, I could hear Him speaking into my soul, telling me that it was okay, that He is there for me. Well, my response was not gratefulness. I was too foolish at the time to know what I was saying. I said, "Yes, Lord, I know you are here for me, but I want someone who I can see, who can give me a real hug, someone who is physically here for me." I was longing for a male companion who would be mine, someone who could hold me as I cried. It may sound crazy, but I felt the Lord's sadness at my response. I was too young and foolish to know what I was doing and saying, but it didn't cause it to hurt less. The Lord gave me exactly what I wanted. I was only eighteen years old when God orchestrated the day I met my husband. He had every single attribute that I had written that I wanted in a husband.

Fast forward back to that night, as I lay in bed weeping like a baby, that day replayed in my mind as though someone had stored that tape recording only to replay it at that very moment. Here I was crying again years later, and I had the man right beside me, and he could not comfort me. He was fast asleep, he did not even stir. The sound of my silent tears did not move him, and I wept even more. My heart was completely broken. For the first time, I really saw how I hurt the Lord and how in His loving way, He did not turn his back on me. He gave me exactly what I wanted, knowing that one day – on that day – I would realize that the man lying beside me was who I wanted, but not who I needed. I could do nothing else but cry, and repent. I needed the Lord's forgiveness so desperately in that moment. He did not hold out on me. When I opened my mouth to say how sorry I was, He opened his arms and accepted me. His love enveloped me like a flood. Encounters like that will begin to minimize the hole in our hearts until it is completely filled with God's love; His amazing, indescribable love.

You Are a Precious Flower

Jeremiah 31:3 says:

The Lord hath appeared of old unto me, saying, Yea,
I have loved thee with an everlasting love: therefore
with lovingkindness have I drawn thee.

There are many other similar passages of Scripture where God reassures us of His love for us. But what is better than a personal demonstration of that love? If you ask me, nothing. I dare you to begin to seek the Lord. I promise you will find Him, and so much more than you ever imagined was possible. You don't have to know about God through only stories you have read or heard about Him because He does want you to know Him on an intimate, personal level. He wants to be the lover of your soul.

The day started out as any ordinary day – don't they all? But it was a time in my life when I was sick and tired of the small amount of money I was making, and I needed more. I was desperate for a new job, a promotion, or even a second job. I asked the manager of a vacant position in my company if she would look at my resume and consider me for an interview. I did this despite the fact that she was extremely unapproachable and hardly ever wore a smile. I did it even though the only qualifications on my resume were my nine CSEC subjects; I was proud of them, but they hardly screamed promotion-worthy. The manager politely agreed and told me to send my resume to her. I sent her my resume, hoped for the best, and then forgot all about it, but I ended up wishing that I hadn't.

Hours later, I walked into the lunch room only to see a table full of heads turn to get a good look at me. I suspect they wanted to match the face to the name of the audacious young lady who would dare apply for such a prestigious position with not even a first degree to her name. As every head turned in unison to look at me, I knew I was the subject of their discussion, and I was almost certain I saw a few people snickering. If there was ever a moment in my life that I had hoped the ground would open up and swallow me whole, it was then. My appetite left immediately, and as I turned to leave the lunchroom, I knew I had to get out of sight fast before anyone saw me crying. I dashed into a private room and cried. I had never felt so low before. I was always so confident in who I was and never allowed my circumstances or what others thought of me to get me down. That day, I hit the emotional rock bottom. I was so embarrassed because a part of me, somewhere deep down inside agreed with them. *Where do I get off thinking I had a chance to get that position?* In that moment, I believed I was not good enough, that I was not qualified. Have you ever cried so much that you cried yourself to sleep? That was me. Like a baby, I had cried myself to sleep in that little room called the sick bay; reserved for ill staff members. It was in that room that the Lord came to meet me. I knew I wasn't sleeping, but somehow, I wasn't awake either. I found myself in a field of flowers, like a meadow. It was a windy day, and there were flowers in the field. But one flower caught my attention as it danced slowly in the wind. Out of all the flowers, this single flower stood solitary. It was yellow, big, bright, and beautiful. Tears came to my eyes as I recalled that vision because the flower caught my attention, as though it was smiling at me. The more I watched it, the closer it seemed to be coming to me, and as I pondered its grace and beauty and how absolutely stunning it was, I heard His voice. He said, "That's you. You are a flower – beautiful and full of grace, making everyone who comes into your presence happy and enamoured by your beauty. You are a flower, and don't you ever forget that." And just like that, I was wide awake. I sat up in the bed so fast I could not believe it. I started crying for a whole different reason. I could not believe He would come to me right there and then and comfort me in a way that changed my whole outlook, my whole life.

You Are Never Alone

God is your refuge and strength, a very present help in times of trouble (See Psalms 46:1). If your nail broke or if you chose to cut your hair, God knows about it and He cares. You are the apple of His eyes. Today, so many people struggle with self-image and identity issues for various reasons. Whatever your reason or struggle may be, know that you were created in the image of God. You and humankind alike were created as a copy of the Creator. Therefore, all He is and what He can do rests in you as well. You were made uniquely you and are given gifts and talents that will aid you to walk in the purpose you have been created for.

Many people struggle with what their calling or purpose is. If this is you, first begin with a prayer. Everything should begin with prayer because where you can go no further; you invite the Lord to complete what you have started. Next, take a pen and paper – better yet, invest in a journal. Write down what you like to do.

It doesn't have to be anything grand, for example, being good at sports or fashion designing, it could simply be that you like to encourage people, or you like to cook. Come up with practical ways in which you can use those skills for the betterment of God's kingdom. How can you give those likes/talents back to Him?

You are never alone. God's promise to you is that He will never leave or forsake you. I know you have probably heard that phrase a thousand times, but have you ever really stopped to ponder each word individually? Well, you should. What does each word mean separately, and what does each word mean together?

I want you to pray right now. Let the Lord know that you are sorry for all the times you turned your back on Him. Tell Him you know now that only He can fill the emptiness in your soul, and you are inviting Him in right now. No matter how high and mighty we may get, every now and then, we all need to say a prayer like this. Get back to that place where you first met God and humbly ask Him to forgive you and help you stay on the right path with Him.

Can you think of a time in your life when you felt empty, like no one or nothing could help you? God gave you the gift of free will, and He will not barge into your life without an invitation. Give Him one today. You will not regret it.

Chapter 7

The Road Less Travelled

As you delve into your pursuit of happiness, it won't take long for you to realize that everything feels different. Your thinking is being renewed and your mindset has shifted so that you now realize that negativity exhausts you and you no longer have the appetite for it. As a result of this unconscious change in your behavior, you may find that your family begin to accuse you of changing. They won't be able to really put their finger on it because they don't yet know what has changed about you, but one thing is certain, they will know that they don't like it.

Friends who have been riding with you from the beginning will also start to jump the wagon. You will notice they no longer respond to your messages the way they used to or initiate a conversation, and things will be noticeably different. Although this process is going to be a painful one to go through, it is inevitable. This road that you now embark upon is going to be a lonely one because the doorway to your success is small enough to fit only you. All the people you are trying to take with you are not able to fit through the doorway; as a result, you are miserable and so are they.

The minute you realize the problem and decide to do what must be done, it might look like judgment coming from the people who are supposed to be your cheerleaders. I don't want you to be surprised when this happens. When your family and/or friends turn on you, making it seem like wanting better for yourself has become a crime, though you will be hurt, I don't want you to be as shocked as I was. You see, the shock can take a long time to wear off. The shock keeps you temporarily paralyzed and off balance, causing you to waste precious time and slowing you down unnecessarily. You must realize that you will be more valuable to your friends and family once you go and find yourself and then come back for them; way more valuable.

When you travel in an airplane, the flight attendants go through the survival tips on where to find the emergency tools in case something goes wrong. They make sure to tell you that if a disaster strikes, you are to put on your own oxygen mask first before attempting to help anyone with their own mask – even your children. You are of absolutely no use to anyone if you are dead. People may not understand this new journey you are on, and they may not like it. Your friends won't like the fact that certain conversations don't entice you anymore or that you are either sticking to yourself more or hanging out with a different set of people; people you believe can help you get to where you want to be. That's okay. You are the one God gave the vision to – the grand vision of where your life is supposed to be and the abundant life you are called to live – so you cannot expect them to understand your journey. That is why it's the road less travelled. This process of finding yourself, accepting who you are, and seeking to become the person you want to be is a lonely and painful one. Who wants to look in the mirror and see all their demons looking back at them? Most people choose not to look. They either cover their mirrors with a cloth, break them, or refrain from even owning a mirror. To take the steps you must, you have to open your eyes.

One of the hardest things to do is accept and forgive yourself. People talk all the time about accepting others for who they are and forgiving others for what they have done, but they hardly ever talk about accepting and forgiving oneself. I admit, I lost some relationships because of my nasty attitude and 'I'm better than you' ways. When you are young and fighting to stay above the dirt, keeping your self-esteem high looks a whole lot like arrogance and narcissism, and because people start to define you as such, you may start to believe you are that person. Most of it is just a misunderstanding on their part from not understanding your story and misunderstanding on your part as well.

Then there is pride. The Bible says that pride goes before a fall, and this is very true. If you can be bold enough to look into yourself and look back at some of the things you have done or said, you might be able to say, *Yes, I can see why I drove some people away,* and you may even owe those people an apology. On the other side of the fence though, you will have the haters. We hear this term so much, and to be honest, I don't like calling them that anymore because I have grown to understand that the people who seem unhappy that you are happy, who will not celebrate your successes but are quick to listen to your failures, are struggling too. They are struggling to fit in with the status quo but are not yet able to lay pride aside and admit their faults and seek help. Until that happens, you have to work on you, and if no one is willing to wait on you to do so, God is a provider and a restorer.

Trusting God means you believe He will provide you with the right people you need to help you move forward and He can and will restore any brokenness sustained along the way. The Bible tells us to:

Write the vision, and make it plain upon tables, that he may run that readeth it. (Habakkuk 2:2b).

So many people live a life filled with regrets, never really coming into a full understanding of who they are, and the plan God has for their lives.

My friend, seek to not be like those people. Although you will not see all the way from A to Z, once you get a glimpse of what your purpose is on this earth, run with it, even if no one else is running with you.

Pay Attention to Your Dreams

The backpack on my back felt heavy as I shifted it to suit my comfort. *Where did it come from?* I asked myself as I kept walking forward. I was going somewhere, but I had no idea where. It was dark, and as I took the time to really look around my surroundings, I realized that the place I was in was creepy. It was like something out of a horror movie. You know the scenes where the eerie music comes on and the actor is all alone in a scary place. As they walk, you know they are about to die. Yes, I was in that scene, except it wasn't a movie. I was in a dark, narrow place that resembled an alley, and I was afraid.

Despite my fears, I kept moving forward because something told me that I needed to, and as I walked, I became aware that there was someone walking with me. Before my natural reaction of fright could take over, I was filled with an immense sense of peace and security; whoever was walking with me, though I could not see him or her, was not there to harm me.

There was a gate up ahead of me, and as I neared it, I felt even more afraid, but this invisible being walking beside me started speaking to me through my mind. There were no spoken words as He reassured me that He is with me and I must not be afraid. That is when it finally dawned on me that it was the Lord walking with me, and I kept going.

Because I could not see Him, I would sometimes forget that I was not walking alone, and I would allow the spirit of fear to get the better of me. When I came up to the gate, not only was it locked, but there were hundreds of spiders of various sizes and shapes all over the gate. If you know me, then you know that I am scared of all bugs, especially spiders. The thought of even touching that gate in an attempt to go through it was enough to make me want to turn back. As I considered my predicament, a still, small voice who had been quiet all this time, spoke to me again, telling me that I cannot turn back now; I have come too far. Just then I noticed something else was there in the shadows, and as I turned to look at it, I could not make out anything except two huge, red circles. Then it hit me, those were eyes. If the eyes were that big, how much bigger was the body. The revelation suddenly came to me that the thing lurking in the corner was the master spider, the leader of them all, and, yes, it was huge. To say I was extremely terrified would be a gross understatement, as all the ways I was going to die started flashing through my mind. Then I realized that at no point had this big, scary monster lurking in the shadows made any attempt to attack me. That was when it hit me. It was not that the creature did not want to devour me, after all, the way it looked at me confirmed how much it hated me and would like nothing less than to destroy me, but it was afraid of who was with me. That realization made me want to dance. I was like, *Ha, you are not so bad after all.* But that feeling was short-lived when I realized I still had to go through the gate with a million spiders all over it.

I took a few more steps toward the gate – it was either that or go back, and though turning back was a safer choice, it was the cowardly choice. I couldn't disappoint the person who had been walking with me the whole time, encouraging me to go on. Taking a deep breath of feigned courage, I put my hand out to open the gate, but to my despair, the gate was locked. Before I could think of turning back, my invisible companion said, "Go over it." I swallowed all the fear that welled up inside me, closed my eyes to all the spiders protecting this perceived portal to purpose, and I climbed. The spiders went in for a feast. They were all over my body – my face and my arms – and to make matters worse, my backpack got stuck on the gate, giving them more time to do more damage. Since the backpack was stuck and I could not see exactly where, I was forced to open my eyes and face my fears. I looked to see what the bag got stuck on and managed to free it, but not before getting a good look at the dilemma that I was in.

I went over the gate and dropped to the other side. I quickly brushed the spiders off me, doing a little dance to shake them off. I checked to see if I had gotten bitten by the spiders, then looked ahead. I was disturbed by the sight in front of me. I was in a new place. It was lit and looked welcoming as if I had somehow found home. I realized that the place in front of me, as bright as it was, could not be seen from the dark, scary alley that I had just come through. Although I knew my journey was not complete, I had gotten to an oasis in my desert. I had accessed a new level and entered into a new dimension.

I jumped out of my sleep and sat up in bed. My breathing was very heavy, the way it usually is after I get one of those very vivid dreams. Spiders? Giant monster spider? Gate? New place? What did it all mean? I had to write it down because the memories don't stay long.

God will speak to you about where He is taking you. It is important that you practice the habit of writing down everything you see and hear. This will happen in various ways, whether by your dreams, as I have experienced, through clear visions in the daytime, or

Him sending someone to speak over your life; write it down. After writing it down, begin to decipher all of its possible meanings and what God could be saying to you. Take that dream I just shared with you for example. The backpack was a clear sign that I was going somewhere, and by its size, it seemed to be somewhere far. The dark, eeriness of the place suggested that that was not a place many people went to and, for obvious reasons, it was very scary. My invisible counterpart was the Lord, and that was God, knowing I needed to be reminded that the journey I was embarking on was going to be long, hard and scary, but He would always be right beside me encouraging me on.

When God sees that you need encouragement, He will not leave you lacking. His promise to you is that when you need Him, He will be there. Isaiah 65:24 sums this up perfectly when the Lord said:

And it shall come to pass, that before they call, I will answer; and while they are yet speaking, I will hear.

God wants you to know and believe this with all your heart.

God used spiders to represent the demons that stood in the way of my purpose. Not only do I have a fear of spiders, but I fear all insects to the point where a close encounter with a lizard had me in tears. Why would God use one of my greatest fears to speak to me? Because, like my dreadful fear of spiders and other bugs, I had a fear of demons and the devil and what they could potentially do to me. The master spider could not touch me in the dream, not because of who I was, but because of the One walking with me. You need to know that you must not fear. The devil cannot harm you unless God permits him. There is peace because if God permits it, then you know it will be for His glory and you will overcome.

The little spiders guarding the gate you are to climb over are only there to scare you away, to cause you to turn back and run away from your divine calling. God loves to speak to us when the noise around us has quieted and when the hustle and bustle of our busy days have halted, and often, He will speak to you through your dreams. However, keep in mind that the devil is an imitator of God, so there are times when you will also have dreams, but they are not from God. Although some dreams may be very clear, the key to differentiating between them is prayer. Always pray and ask God if the dream is from Him and to reveal its meaning to you.

You have this amazing, unrestricted access to the King of kings, so don't forget to use it. Do not be overcome with fear, but instead overcome fear by standing on the promises of the God who has continued to prove himself over and over again. God says:

Fear thou not; for I am with thee: be not dismayed;
for I am thy God: I will strengthen thee; yea,
I will help thee; yea, I will uphold thee with the
right hand of my righteousness. (Isaiah 41:10).

These are powerful words, and this promise will fuel you to climb over all your closed gates, spiders and all, if you only hold dear to it.

To Drop and Be Dropped

When you think about the things holding you back, some people will come to your mind. You will start to have convictions on a daily basis about the people in your life. You may tell yourself that being around them is good for you and that you can help change them, but instead, they are changing you, and not for the better. Why? Because sin is sweet, and the flesh is all about pleasure. If you are human, you are going to be drawn to pleasure. Therefore, playing this game of being on the fence and compromising your faith so as not to offend anyone is a dangerous one.

Many of us get drawn away as a result of compromising. Do not try to hold on to both lives by having a foot on each side; that is what I tried to practice. I eventually had to make the decision to let go of someone I had considered a good friend. We had lots of fun together but when I decided to answer God's call, my spirit was constantly grieved within me. Although the person was a nice person, she had her lifestyle, and as a result of us being friends, I was expected to share in that lifestyle, even if it went against my faith. The things that enticed her, that used to entice me, no longer did, and being with her started to feel like a struggle. That was a fight between flesh and spirit. The Bible talks about this in the very first chapter of the book of Psalms:

Blessed is the man that walketh not in the counsel of the ungodly, nor standeth in the way of sinners, nor sitteth in the seat of the scornful. (Psalm 1:1)

Do not let people shame you into believing you are not a Christian and you are judging people because of your choice to depart from those who live very different lives from the new one you are trying to live now. It is the Word of God, and, yes, though you will need to commune with sinners in order to introduce them to God, you have to self-assess. Are you strong enough not to be influenced or easily led astray to do things you will regret later? I wasn't, so I had to make the tough decision to leave that friendship.

If there are people you love very much, but it is always a struggle when you hang out with them, then you have an important decision to make. Familiarize yourself with the truth of God's Word, such as Proverbs 12:26:

*The righteous is more excellent than his neighbour:
but the way of the wicked seduceth them.*

Also, Proverbs 27:17:

*Iron sharpeneth iron; so a man sharpeneth
the countenance of his friend.*

Say goodbye to the kind of people who will lead you astray. It may not look like it now, but they will forgive you, and you will find that as they grow more and more unhappy with their way of life, you will become a beacon for them, someone to turn to and help them begin their journey to freedom.

There will be some relationships you hold on to thinking they are the ones who support your journey and are good influences. However, you find out that they won't be joining you on your new faith-walk either, except for totally different reasons. While you kept them around, they decide to drop you. Be prepared for the shock and grieve if you must. It is a normal part of the process. Some of those relationships were with people you considered your ride or die people, and it will feel as though you are experiencing a death in the family. I have had cases where my friends have stopped talking to me completely, and when I asked them what I did, they were unable to give me an answer. Whether it was their mistake or not, I want you to learn to consider all things as God's doing; His handiwork. You will be tempted to hold on to those people, but they are the ones you need to let go of.

I have had people I considered as dear friends come to my wedding one week and the next, they no longer spoke to me. There was no disagreement or tension, just a disappearance. For me, there is no way to explain it, except to say it must be God's doing. I encourage you to begin thinking this way. It is all a part of God's plan.

When the Lord is in full control of your life, then you can rest in any situation, knowing that He must have allowed it to happen for a reason. You must understand that many of our friends and loved ones are struggling the same way we are. They are struggling with self-identity and self-acceptance. In today's world where it's all about putting your best face forward on Facebook, Instagram, and other popular social media sites, everyone is trying to give the best representation of themselves. It takes something extra to stand up and say, "I am not perfect; I am not happy. How can I truly achieve joy in my life without having to filter it?" As the people you love make their own choices to walk away from you, cry if you must. Be mad if you must, and go through your process, but after all is said and done, do not hold it against them. I believe this is what God wanted for us when He encouraged us to pray for those who persecute us and to bless our enemies. They are struggling, and if you can manage to humble yourself, put away your pride, and pray that they begin to experience the peace that you now have, then it would all be worth it, for both them and you.

So, however it happens, whether you had to drop some people, or you had some people drop you, rejoice nonetheless, because if you believe that our God is a restorer, you never know who might be waiting around the corner on the road less travelled.

Chapter 8

Ditch the Coward – Move Your Life Forward!

Today, it is the popular thing for everyone to say *Nobody's perfect* or *I am only human*. While these are true, most of us believe them because it lets us off the hook. If we were honest with ourselves, we are fearful of a lot of things, especially the truth; especially when we find out that everything we believed about ourselves for so long are lies.

You have the power to erase those lies and replace them with the truth. Lies such as *You are ugly* can be replaced with *I am beautiful, uniquely, and wonderfully made*. Lies such as *You are worthless and will never amount to anything* can be replaced with truths such as *You are priceless*, and *You can do all things through Christ who strengthens you*. I dare you to find out what will happen when you decide to release the lies and hold on to the truth. Do not let yourself off the hook and remain in a life that is less than perfect. God calls you into perfection. He tells us to be perfect, even as our Father in Heaven is perfect (See Matthew 5:48). Those words sound like such big shoes to fill, so unattainable, but you can do it. You can do all things through the power of Jesus Christ, who is your strength, and in your weakness, His power is made strong. God will never ask you to do anything that He has not already equipped you to do.

After a life of so many ups and downs, many battles won and lost; I am determined to keep moving forward. All my life I had to fight for what I wanted and to get to where I needed to go. No one is going to hand you your future well-decorated on a platter. You cannot go on

Amazon.com or your favourite online store and order 'a good life' for yourself. You must make that happen. When God says in Deuteronomy 30:19: *I call heaven and earth to record this day against you, that I have set before you life and death, blessing and cursing: therefore choose life, that both thou and thy seed may live:* He meant it. You don't get to quit. You don't get to bow out or throw in the towel; failure is not an option, because the God you serve tells you He has already overcome the world. He says you are more than a conqueror and you have already won the victory. You cannot lose, unless you give up.

Today, the suicide rate among young adults is so high, because young people are struggling mentally and need help. Somewhere along the line, they have been led to believe that if they ended their life, it will be better for them and for everyone else involved. Anyone thinking this way couldn't be more wrong. First, life will not and cannot be any better for them because they are dead – and suicide is a big slap in the face of the One who blew that life into their body to begin with. It is also not beneficial to the people who they leave behind because those people are left broken-hearted and confused. They are left with the high and unnecessary cost of planning a funeral. In addition to that, if they somehow thought they were spiting anyone by killing themselves, the truth is, life goes on, and sooner or later, they will only be a memory. It sounds harsh, I know, but tough love is still love. Do not give up on this beautiful gift you are given called life. Your best days are still ahead, and you are going to overcome.

Stand Up For Yourself

People will love you as much as they can use you because, by nature, human beings have become selfish, putting themselves and their own desires ahead of everything else. We have been trained to believe that it is a dog-eat-dog world and it is survival of the fittest. As a result, we get caught up in the rat race, working harder to have things that we will never have time to enjoy, and allowing ourselves to be used and abused by others to get to somewhere we don't really want to go.

Do not become someone who works hard their whole life, climbing the perceived ladder of success, only to finally reach the top and realize that you were going up the wrong ladder all along. Instead, become someone who makes it their goal to find what is right for you. Take some time to think about what you like to do, what you are passionate about, and find the courage to go after it. Stand up for yourself too because on your journey, you will come across a lot of people on the same narrow path, and if they can use you as a stepping stone to get ahead, they will. Be honest enough with yourself to ask, *Am I allowing this person, this job, or whatever it is to use me?* Yes, it is easier said than done because we are called to strike the perfect balance. We are called to love our enemies and to give, and so we do just that in obedience. Why then do we feel so burned out and full of resentment in the end? I believe it is because we are fuelling other people – their goals and dreams, giving them all of us without ever receiving anything back. In order to achieve perfect balance, we must remember our source. Who or what is your gas station when you run out of fuel to keep going? Your refuelling is in your worship, it is in your praise, and in knowing your true self-worth. When you know your worth, you can stand up for yourself and feel good about the results, come what may.

Years ago, on one of my very first jobs, I was working in a temporary capacity. At the time, my wages were about fourteen thousand Jamaican dollars per fortnight. Even though I was a young girl, I had all the responsibilities of an adult. I was helping my mother with the rent and utilities; I had to find transportation back and forth to work; and I had to eat. At first, I was so excited for an opportunity to do some work and be rewarded accordingly, that I allowed myself to be used. I was not receiving what I deserved, but I was grateful.

There is a time for everything under the sun, and seasons change. You must become the meteorologist of your own life to know when the seasons have changed and how to adjust your sail accordingly. So, after a time, when not getting enough was no longer enough, I decided to do something about it. I knew I wasn't being paid properly because I could not pay my bills, let alone buy clothes for myself. I was constantly broke, borrowing from he, she, and the old lady, and I wanted out of it. I went to the necessary heads of department to ask for a raise. Not surprisingly, I was told in the most diplomatic of ways that the company was not in such a position, and I would have to be given more to do to earn that increase. The tears came. When you are at the end of your road, tears will become a new normal for you, but do not give up. Part of knowing your true self-worth is knowing what you deserve, and when others are not willing to give you what you deserve, fight for it nevertheless.

After many meetings and emails with Human Resources and different Managers, nothing changed. The answer was still no, but I was desperate. Desperation will stand firm and look you in the face, wanting to know if you wanted it bad enough, and I did. So, I did what many would not have done. I went ahead and booked a meeting with the person sitting at the top of the Human Resources ladder – my boss's boss's boss. I knew all the people I had spoken to previously would not have appreciated my actions, but I wanted what was mine too badly to care.

After being granted the rare opportunity to have this meeting, I laid out all that was on my heart. I had been temporary in that particular position for over two years, and as a result of the temporary status, I did not get proper health insurance benefits, no clothing or lunch allowance, and I was not being paid by the same principles used to pay the permanently employed. The position I held would be needed for a long time, and it was not fair to keep me in a position where I was given a contract that would be constantly expiring and renewed. In the end, the boss made a couple of phone calls to the same people I had been having meetings with for the past months, and in no time, I was signing my new permanent contract. What I did was risky and could have easily cost me my job, but

I was successful in getting what I deserved. You must be willing to take risk when fighting for what is yours.

No one else is responsible to give you the life you want for yourself and the life you know you deserve. That responsibility is yours. Proverbs 28:1, one of my personal favourites, tells us that:

The wicked flee when no man pursueth:
but the righteous are bold as a lion.

Your job is to remain righteous. Seek out what God commands you to do in order to live a righteous life and do your best to live that life – in public and behind closed doors. God says whatever you do in private, He will reward you openly (See Matthew 6:6). That will make the difference in your story because where your strength stops, God will pick up where you left off and finish what you started.

God's Anointing Is On You, Go Forth and Conquer!

You will encounter many ups and downs on this journey. God did not promise that the road would be easy, but He did promise to be with you every single step of the way. You must understand and accept that, knowing you have an advocate in Christ Jesus. Jesus Christ died and rose again, so you can have this amazing privilege of a relationship with Him, which is the most intimate one of all.

There was a time when I would pray earnestly to see God's face. I knew that the Old Testament said that you cannot see God's face and live, but that was before Jesus came into the world, and I started having this deep desire to see God. I wanted to see the One I had fallen in love so deeply with, and I found myself praying, "Lord, I want you to come to me. I want to see you. I want to go deeper with you." I had heard too many Christians talk about their own experiences where the Lord audibly spoke to them or visited them. At first, I did not believe it. I was sceptical, but the truth is, I was a little scared. What if it was true and the Lord does visit people in that way? So, I began to desire Him more, and my words began to change.

The Bible tells us to delight in the Lord, and He will give us the desires of our heart (See Psalm 37:4). I cannot say I prayed specifically to see God's face all the time, but I know it had become one of the deep desires of my heart. Then, it started happening. I would get a weird feeling every time it got quiet in my house or when I was alone. I felt like someone was there with me, and I was feeling His presence getting stronger each time. I would wake up at 3 a.m., almost every morning for no apparent reason, with the Lord on my mind. It began happening so frequently and consistently that I became terrified. It got to a point where I would want to go to the bathroom, but I was so afraid to take a corner and see Jesus, that I would lie in bed until my bladder complained. I wasn't even living alone, I lived with my husband, but those thoughts and the fear only came when he was asleep. I was walking around my house on tiptoes expecting to see someone at any minute. I was that sure in my spirit that I was going to see the Lord. There was also doubt, and I tried to talk myself out of my wild thoughts: *Oh, you're crazy, go to bed*, etc. This went on for about two weeks until I couldn't take it anymore.

After one more 3 a.m. bathroom episode where I was almost deathly afraid of going, I decided that I could not keep doing that. I sat on my toilet and spoke to the Lord. I said, "Lord Jesus, if you're going to visit me, please don't frighten me, because I'm feeling really scared." That was my prayer before I climbed back into bed.

The nights following were seemingly back to normal. I was sleeping more, and I believed I had put the idea behind me once and for all, but then it happened. I was on my side of the bed sleeping like a baby, my husband was on his side, and our daughter – who was probably one year old at the time – was sleeping in her crib. I knew it was not a dream. Have you ever been sleeping, and someone came and stood over you? Whether it was their shadow or a human's innate ability to sense when another person is in a room, you knew someone was standing there. I knew someone was standing in front of me, so I opened my eyes. Standing there in all His glory was the Lord Jesus. I could not believe it. The first thing He said to me as He spoke through His mind to mine was, "See, I didn't frighten you." I did not know how or in what form He would come, but I knew with all my heart that He was going to. He took the time to prepare me for His visitation. I believe He did that so when it happened, I would know for a fact that I was not dreaming. The only way I can describe what I saw was that looking at Him was like looking at a man engrossed in light. I could tell it was Him, but I couldn't tell the color of His hair or His eyes or even the color of His skin. He was glowing all over, and my room came alive with His glory.

Naturally, if the Lord Jesus is standing in your room, what do you do? You want to get up and talk to Him, right? I'm sure you would have a million questions and things you were dying to know. It was the exact same for me. As I struggled to sit up, the Lord spoke to me again and said, "No, don't get up." I could tell He was not a man of many words, and as He spoke, the love that poured out of His very gaze was so enthralling. I would describe it as liquid love, poured all over me like oil from the head to the toes. When He spoke, His eyes smiled, as my heart, mind, and soul heard Him clearly. We didn't need words – this was He who I described as the lover of my soul. My whole being – body, mind, and soul – was created by Him. He knew me in the deepest of ways – there was no secret hidden from Him. As I wondered why He came, I noticed He had something in His hands. I don't know if it had just appeared there or if I hadn't noticed it before, but the only way I can describe the *thing* in His hands is that it was like a ball of light, liquid and solid at the same time. Then He did the very thing He came to do; He bent over me and placed that *thing* inside of me; He gave it to me. I could literally feel when it entered my body, my chest, even as I wondered what it was. I was going crazy wanting to do my own thing, to talk to Him, to hug Him, to just sit up in bed, but He wouldn't let me. Once He placed His 'gift' within me, He hushed me back to sleep. His final words to me that day has given me the courage to actually be writing this particular testimony. I have replayed those words over and over in my own head to convince myself that I was not dreaming and not going insane. He said, "When you wake up in the morning, don't let anyone or anything tell you that this was a dream." I live by those words; I hold on to them dearly. If I remember nothing else, I remember the Lord's final words to me. Writing this now, I take the risk of being judged and accused of lying because I believe God more. As He told me to go back to sleep, I had no choice or power to disobey. It was as though a spirit of sleep came upon me. As I drifted off back to sleep, I remember distinctly that my final thoughts were, *I cannot wait to tell Dain this in the morning!* Sure enough, when I woke up in the morning, my first words to my husband were, "Dain, Jesus came to me last night!" and I excitedly shared what happened with him.

The Bible is filled with so many miraculous stories. So many things have been written down that if we saw those things happening today, it would be hard for us to believe. The stories written down are about who God is and the things He has done, for example, healing the sick, raising the dead, parting the Red Sea. So many amazingly impossible things to the human mind.

You will find so much unbelief and scepticism surrounding your belief in God. Do not be surprised when you find it among people who also call themselves believers in God and followers of Christ.

My friend, there is so much deception in the world today that I want you to put on your top five list of prayer requests that God will guard you against deception, even guard you against deceiving your own self. Jeremiah 17:9 states that:

The heart is deceitful above all things, and desperately wicked: who can know it?

I encourage you to pray against deception.

The book of Matthew speaks about people who said they were followers of Christ, who did 'Christian-like' things, yet:

Not every one that saith unto me, Lord, Lord, shall enter into the kingdom of heaven; but he that doeth the will of my Father which is in heaven. (Matthew 7:21).

There are people who will hear God say:

I never knew you: depart from me, ye that work iniquity. (Matthew 7:23b)

If you remember nothing else, remember to care more about what God thinks about you rather than people. Seek earnestly the approval of your Heavenly Father. He knew you before you were conceived, and He has the blueprint for your life laid out before Him.

As you embark on this journey of uprooting all the weeds from your life in order to allow your roots to spread, know that you came from the dirt for a reason. Your circumstances and some people tried to bury you, but they didn't know you are a seed. I charge you to go forth and bloom!

About the Author

Collena Doctor was raised in a single-parent home along with her three siblings. Although they did not have much, their mother ensured that they were raised with understanding and their own sense of self-worth. Although she sometimes went to bed without dinner, to school without lunch money and had to learn without textbooks, Collena quickly learned how to make the most of everything she had been given. Soon, she would top all her classes, and was placed on the Honour Roll at her school every year, eventually graduating as one of the top students in her graduating class. Her story is one of resilience and perseverance, which declares to young people that it is not how you start, but how you choose to finish. Collena fervently believes that instead of complaining, one should aim to break the chains of poverty, low standards and unfulfilled dreams that threaten to hold us hostage.

Today, Collena is a wife, mother, Motivational Speaker, Certified Christian Life Coach, and founder of the Women of Worth Christian Life-Coaching for Upliftment and Business (the WOWCLUB). She speaks specifically on the area of self-worth because it is her belief that once we become aware of who we are, and who God has called us to be, we will then be equipped with the tools needed to fight our way out of the darkness, and into His marvellous light. It is her passion to help young women to succeed in life by understanding that knowing our worth, aids in finding our rightful place in the Earth.

To learn more about Collena Doctor,
The WOWCLUB, and to subscribe to her Blog, visit
www.collenadoctor.com.